Her Birth and Later Years

....

WESLEYAN POETRY

Also by Irena Klepfisz

POETRY

periods of stress (1975)

Keeper of Accounts (1982)

Different Enclosures: Poetry and Prose of Irena Klepfisz (1985)

A Few Words in the Mother Tongue:
Poems Selected and New, 1971–1990 (1990)

PROSE

Dreams of an Insomniac: Jewish Feminist Essays, Speeches,
and Diatribes (1990)

CO-EDITOR

with Melanie Kaye/Kantrowitz, *A Tribe of Dina:*
A Jewish Woman's Anthology (1986)

with Rita Falbel and Donna Nevel, *Jewish Women's Call for Peace:*
A Handbook for Jewish Women on the Israeli/Palestinian Conflict (1990)

with Daniel Soyer, *The Stars Bear Witness:*
The Jewish Labor Bund 1897–2017 (2017)

Irena Klepfisz

Her Birth
and Later Years

New and
Collected Poems,
1971–2021

WESLEYAN UNIVERSITY PRESS
MIDDLETOWN, CONNECTICUT

Wesleyan University Press
Middletown CT 06459
www.wesleyan.edu/wespress

First paperback edition 2024
Paperback ISBN 978-0-8195-0108-0
Typeset in Arno Pro by Passumpsic Publishing
Manufactured in the United States of America

Some of the poems in this volume first appeared in
A Few Words in the Mother Tongue: Poems Selected and New, 1971–1990
(Eighth Mountain Press, 1990).

Versions of a number of the most recent poems appeared originally in
Jewish Socialist, The Manhattan Review, In geveb: A Journal of Yiddish Studies, Sinister Wisdom, The Georgia Review, The Progressive, and
Jewish American Poetry: Poems, Commentary and Reflections.

Cover art: Judith Waterman, *Untitled,* oil on canvas, 8 ft. × 11 ft.

The Library of Congress cataloged the hardcover edition as:
Names: Klepfisz, Irena, 1941– author.
Title: Her birth and later years: new and collected poems, 1971–2021/
    Irena Klepfisz.
Description: Middletown, Connecticut: Wesleyan University Press, [2022]
Series: Wesleyan poetry | Includes index. | Summary: "The collected
    poems of Irena Klepfisz, a feminist, lesbian, Holocaust survivor, and
    scholar of the Yiddish language. These powerful, searching poems move
    easily between personal, historical, and political, demonstrating the
    singularity of Klepfisz's work as a vital American voice." — Provided
    by publisher.
Identifiers: LCCN 2022016278 (print) | LCCN 2022016279 (ebook) |
    ISBN 9780819500168 (cloth) | ISBN 9780819500175 (ebook)
Subjects: BISAC: POETRY/American/General | SOCIAL SCIENCE/
    Jewish Studies | LCGFT: Poetry.
Classification: LCC PS3561.L388 H47 2022 (print) | LCC PS3561.L388
    (ebook) | DDC 811/.54—dc23/eng/20220607
LC record available at https://lccn.loc.gov/2022016278
LC ebook record available at https://lccn.loc.gov/2022016279

5 4 3 2 1

In memory of
painter extraordinaire
partner and lifelong companion
JUDITH WATERMAN
1936–2014

Contents

....

Early Work (1971)

Searching for my Father's Body	3
The Widow and Daughter	7

from *periods of stress* (1975)

I

during the war	13
p o w s	14
herr captain	15
death camp	17
about my father	18
perspectives on the second world war	19

II

conditions	22
periods of stress	24
please don't touch me	25
dinosaurs and larger issues	27
when the heart fails	34
it was good	35
flesh is cold	36
they're always curious	37
they did not build wings for them	38
the fish	41

III

in between	44
the house	45
blending	48
edges	49

IV

    aesthetic distance   56
    self-dialogues   57

Two Sisters: Helen and Eva Hesse (1978)

    An Introduction   63
    Two Sisters: A Monologue   65

Keeper of Accounts (1982)

I From the Monkey House and Other Cages
    Monkey 1   76
    Monkey 2   87
II Different Enclosures
    Contexts   98
    Work Sonnets/with Notes and a Monolgue about a Dialogue
        I. Work Sonnets   104
        II. Notes   113
        III. A Monologue about a Dialogue   115
    A Poem for Judy/beginning a new job   118
III Urban Flowers
    Mnemonic Devices: Brooklyn Botanic Gardens, 1981   122
    Royal Pearl   124
    Lithops   125
    Aesthetics   126
    Winter Light   127
    Oleander   128
    Cactus   129
    Abutilon in Bloom   130
IV Inhospitable Soil
    Glimpses of the Outside
        A place   132
        A visit   136
        A place in time   140
        Mourning   143

Bashert
 These words are dedicated to those who died   145
 These words are dedicated to those who survived   147
 1. Poland, 1944: My mother is walking down a road   148
 2. Chicago, 1964: I am walking home alone at midnight   150
 3. Brooklyn, 1971: I am almost equidistant from
   two continents   153
 4. Cherry Plain, 1981: I have become a keeper of accounts   156
Solitary Acts   159

A Few Words in the Mother Tongue (1983–1990)

I cannot swim   171
Di rayze aheym/The journey home
 1. *Der fentster*/The window   174
 2. *Vider a mol*/Once again   175
 3. *Zi flit*/She flies   176
 4. *A beys-oylem*/A cemetery   177
 5. *Kashes*/Questions   178
 6. *Zi shemt zihk*/She is ashamed   179
 7. *In der fremd*/Among strangers   180
 8. *Di tsung*/The tongue   181
 9. *Di rayze aheym*/The journey home   182
Etlekhe verter oyf mame-loshn/A few words in the
 mother tongue   183
Fradel Schtok   186
Der mames shabosim/My Mother's Sabbath Days   188
'67 Remembered   190
Warsaw, 1983: *Umschlagplatz*   193
East Jerusalem, 1987: *Bet Shalom* (House of Peace)   195

Her Birth and Later Years (1990–2021)

Footnotes
 March 1939: Warsaw, Poland   202
 Warsaw, 1941: The story of her birth   204

Pesakh: Reynolda Gardens, Winston-Salem
    1. Winter 210
    2. Spring 211
    3. The seder table 212
Mitsrayim: Goat Dream 213
Der soyne/The Enemy: An Interview in Gaza ... 216
In memory of Razan al-Najjar 217
Instructions of the dying elder 221
Dearest Friend: Regarding Esther Frumkin 224

Millet's *Flight of Crows*

Five ways to view a drawing 228

Mourning Cycle

Parsing the question 234
This House 235
Liberation of the roses 237
trees 238
wound: a memory 239
Wind chime 240
Grief changes   and doesn't 241
Entering the stream 242
between shadow and night: a treatise on loneliness ... 243

And Death Is Always with Us

For Jean Swallow: whom I barely knew 250
My mother at 99: Looking for home 253
my mother's loveseat 255
July 22: Geology 256
Jamaica Wildlife Preserve: September 258

from The old poet cycle

    The old poet   reconsiders acting   260

    The old poet   tries unsuccessfully to bring

        chaos   back into her order   262

    The old poet   and Orion   263

    The old poet's   become tired   264

The old poet remembers   the immigrant girl   265

Grief: Brunswick Public Library, Maine   267

Der fremder in der fremd   269

Acknowledgments   271

Glossary   273

Notes   275

Index of titles   277

Early Work

$\left(1971\right)$

Searching for my Father's Body

Searching for my father's body
I begin with the index
hoping to see the name
and to catch sight of a familiar grave.

It all depends on who you knew,
or rather who knew of you,
that determines history;
which circle self-conscious
wanted to commit to paper
its existence and mark a common grave.

The shock of not finding his name
is always the same. Unused to his
anonymity, I close the books angry
that his body was not discovered
and remains buried in an unmarked grave.

It is more painful
when there is no index.
I put it off, thinking
there's time, he's been
buried for twenty-eight years;
one more day won't make a difference.

I numb myself and begin the body check
skimming quickly unwilling to be caught
in strangers' tragedies, only looking directly
at those whom I would have known
had circumstances been different.

The search leaves me weak.
I am still not hardened.
Often caught by a particular sight
I begin to read, despite myself,
and learn a new name, another event,
still another atrocity. I smell again
the burning bodies, see the flames,
wade through sewers in a last desperate effort,
till some present distraction,
like hunger or cold, draws
me back and I begin closing windows
and preparing dinner.

After dinner I procrastinate.
Again I ask myself: should I really do this
and if I do it, will it finally
be done with? Once having found him,
will I be able to leave him in his grave
or will I still insist on carrying
him with me, a thirty-year-old man
whom I never knew?
Will I finally purge myself of the last image
he presented to his friends
when he chose deliberately, in split-
second consciousness, his own style of dying?

> In one of the attics we are suddenly surrounded. Nearby in the same
> attic are the Germans and it is impossible to reach the stairs. In the dark
> corners of the attic we cannot even see one another. We do not notice
> Sewek Dunski and Junghajzer who crawl up the stairs from below, reach
> the attic, get behind the Germans, and throw a grenade. We do not even
> pause to consider how it happens that Michał Klepfisz jumps straight
> onto the German machine pistol firing from behind the chimney. We
> only see the cleared path. After the Germans have been thrown out,
> several hours later, we find Michał's body perforated like a sieve from
> two machine-pistol series.[1]

Confusing details, difficult to follow,
but the main fact, his death,
stares at me from the faded page,
stares at me without penetrating
my reason or understanding.
Simply a fact, dead,
like the object it describes.

I am dissatisfied. I am angry.
I would have liked more life
in this description.
I would have liked those present
to have stopped (*We do not even pause*),
to have examined the body,
to have made sure no pulse was there
(*We only see the cleared path*),
to have described his stillness, their certainty
that he was really dead at that moment,
that they hadn't deserted him,
that he didn't lie there alone,
feeling his own death.

I want more details
to fill up my emptiness.

> But the fighting had only begun. On Shwentoyerska Street it raged around
> the brush factories. A group under the command of Michel Klepfisz [sic]
> took a heavy toll of Germans. They battled for every building and for
> every floor of every building. They fought along the stairways until they
> were forced to the top floors. Then the Germans usually set fire to the
> building. Our fighters would dash through prepared openings in the attic
> walls to begin the fight again in the adjoining building.
>   On the fifth day [sic] of battle, in executing such a withdrawal,
> Michel's group found themselves caught in an attic with German soldiers.
> In the dark, the fighting was confused. A German machine gun held
> Michel's men at bay by sweeping their side of the attic from behind a
> chimney.
>   Two comrades managed to get close enough to the main body of Nazis
> to throw a hand grenade. At that precise moment, Michel hurled himself
> on the machine gun. It stopped firing.
>   An hour later, when the Germans were cleared out, his comrades found
> Michel's body with two neat rows of bullet holes across the stomach.[2]

I do not want this death.
Instead I leap towards life
when my father
slept

> *Michał himself, thanks to a Polish acquaintance and worker and the
> two Pepesowske sisters (Marysha Sawicka and Anna Michalska) whom
> he had drawn into the work to help Jewish underground fighters, was
> able to find places where he could stay overnight, and when all doors
> were hermetically sealed and it was impossible to find a roof over his
> head, he would go to sleep in the cemetery among the graves.*[3]

in Christian cemeteries,
perhaps even in the one
where his sister,
who succumbed in a hospital,
lay buried
under a Christian name.

And my father
sleeps among the graves
in Christian cemeteries
grateful
that there is a dry spell,
that the contact will have a pistol,
that he will be able to jump the wall,
that perhaps tomorrow Marysha
will find him a real place to sleep.
It is here I see him most clearly
as he sleeps leaning against a tombstone
and dreams, never considering
where he himself will one day be buried.

1. Marek Edelman, *The Ghetto Fights*, translated from the Polish by Zofia Nalkowsak.
(Łódź: Central Committee of the Bund).

2. Bernard Goldstein, *The Stars Bear Witness*, translated from the Yiddish by Leonard
Shatzkin (New York: Viking Press, 1949).

3. I. S. Hertz, *Doyres Bundistn* (New York: *Undzer tsayt farlag*), quotation cited trans-
lated by Irena Klepfisz.

The Widow and Daughter

"The widow Rose and small daughter Irena
survived and now reside in New York."
Translated from the Yiddish in *Doyres
Bundistn* (Generations of Bundists)

The widow
a shadow of the wife Rose
    (he was over six feet
    and called her *Mała,*
    little one)
at one time expected
to live
not survive.

In those days
she was romantic
    (they met one winter
    when he chased
    and overtook her on a ski slope).
She read many novels,
knew all the love songs
    (one in particular
    was her favorite —
    ja nie jestem winna,
    it's not my fault)
knew the first part
of *Pan Tadeusz* by heart,
helped her husband
with his work
    (he was an engineer
    and she drew circles for him
    with a protractor)

and never believed
that he might die
    (he was a champion jumper
    and discus thrower)
but would be young always
in their apartment in Warsaw
    (it was sometimes called
    she told me proudly
    the little Paris of Eastern Europe)
where she would receive her sisters,
nieces, nephews (one of the twins died)
and dreamed into a mist even grandchildren
of unborn sons and daughters
and looked forward to intellectual discussions
about the progress of the workers' movement,
the latest romance in a novel or the family.

Instead she survived
motherhood
    (she was in labor for three days,
    then he said: something has to be done)
the Aryan side
    (she became a maid
    and was polishing silver for *them*
    while the ghetto burned)
widowhood
    (as a child I asked
    if she cried a lot
    when they told her
    and she said
    yes)
and finally New York
    (she became a dressmaker
    and did alterations)
with the little daughter
product of three days of labor
a moving monument
whose melted existence
formed an eternal flame
(at memorial meetings
she lit candles
for all the children
who had perished).

These two:
widow and half-orphan
survived and now resided
in a three-room apartment
with an ivy-covered fire escape
which at night
clutched like a skeleton
at the child's bedroom wall.

To this apartment
which chained them
welded them
in a fatal embrace
the missing one
returned at night.

The missing one
was surely
the most
    important
link.

He held out on the fire escape
refusing to give up
his strategic position.
He was there
on the wall
with his whole family
staring out of the picture,
on the piano
staring out of the picture,
in the living room
(vying with her mother for attention)
staring out of the picture,
till the apartment
seemed to burst with his eyes
which penetrated every corner
seizing every movement of their mouths
and made them conscious
that he understood
every word they spoke.

And when the two crowded
into the kitchen at night
he would press himself between them
pushing, thrusting, forcing them to remember,
even though he had made his decision,
had chosen his own way
rather than listening to the pleas of her silence
    (she once said: I never complained about his activities
    and Michał said he was glad I was not like other wives
    who wanted to draw their husbands back into safety)
he would press himself between them —
hero and betrayer
legend and deserter —
so when they sat down to eat
they could taste his ashes.

from *periods of stress*

(1975)

I
....

during the war
germans were known
to pick up infants
by their feet
swing them through the air
and smash their heads
against plaster walls.

somehow
i managed
to escape that fate.

pows

the p o w s came home   some after
seven years   a long time to return to
a wife   suddenly reaching   her menopause
a daughter   menstruating   every month
it's a hard lesson   to understand:
wrinkled thighs   and sagging breasts

my father came home   to me   for the first time
in twenty-nine years   just last night   in a
dream   he was old   and tired
and so scarred so very unlike   the image
i have of him   he pulled his hat   down
over his eyes   ashamed   of his years   his shabbiness
and waited   on the staircase   hoping   i'd say
welcome home   dad
                              he was thirty   killed
by a german   machine gun   defending   the roof
of a brush factory   was declared   a hero
awarded   the highest medal   a soldier could
get awarded   posthumously
                              i am now   almost thirty-
two   should have borne   him a grandson   to carry
his name   he came home   a bit   early

herr captain

i whispered as he came   through the gate
captain i am clean   i've been trained
well   i said   captain   i'm not over
used

he was hard   so hard   forcing bending me
till i could not breathe   slamming against me
my mouth filled with terror   i was pierced
in two   when he suddenly pulled out
my head back   he murmured   what a light rider
my grandmother too   rode her cossack lover
in pain he moaned   harder quicker   ride me now
fearful i ran jumping the gate   with the guards
laughing grimacing through the window   nervous
biting their nails   the dogs barked my legs spread   slapped
around his waist i whipped him further   deeper   till
i felt the blood flooding the field   filling the drowning well
lapping over me   drinking in the smell of his hair
his stomach swollen against me   he collapsed
but i held on   pushing my heels into his back
my teeth clenched i hissed for my grandmother her crooked wig
her gold teeth   and her cossack lover crawling from the well she
pushed up her buttocks as she came over the wall fell to the ground
head first her wig cocked over one eye a butcher knife under her
skirt my mother floats in well water zeyde in mourning tears his red
hair hears them again on the kitchen floor slipping in so smoothly she
was wet from the beginning the horse neighing outside and bobe her
ears pierced at the age of three weeks pulls out the butcher knife
begins slashing till his hands severed he falls back

he brings me soap
his boots are shiny
not like the others   who arrive from the fields
crusted over

In my early teens I read *House of Dolls*, a novel written by a male survivor under the pseudonym Katzetnik 134633 and based on a diary of an anonymous Jewish woman who did not survive the Holocaust. When I rediscovered it, I immediately recognized it as the main unconscious source for "herr captain." Although today I see sexuality and violence from a different perspective than I did in the early 1970s when I wrote it, "herr captain" is to me still relevant as a poem about Jewish women's experiences and survival.

death camp

when they took us   to the shower   i saw
the rebitsin   her sagging breasts   sparse
pubic hairs   i knew   and remembered
the old rebe   and turned   my eyes away
i could still hear   her advice   a woman
with a husband   a scholar

when they turned   on the gas   i smelled
it   first   coming at me   pressed myself
hard to the wall   crying   rebitsin   rebitsin
i am here with you   and the advice you gave me
i screamed   into the wall   as the blood burst from
my lungs   cracking her nails in women's flesh i watched
her capsize   beneath me my blood in her mouth   i screamed

when they dragged my body   into the oven   i burned
slowly at first   i could smell my own flesh   and could
hear   them grunt   with the weight of the rebitsin
and they flung   her on top   of me   and i could smell
her hair burning   against my stomach

when i pressed through   the chimney
it was sunny   and clear   my smoke
was distinct   i rose quiet   left her
beneath

about my father

—he became a teetotaler out of his socialist convictions; during
    the war he began to drink again
—he was casual; he kept his tie in his pocket till the last minute
    before oral exams
—he left me on the street to be picked up by the nuns from the
    orphanage; he watched me from a distant doorway
—once he refused to hit me; he told my mother his hand was
    too large
—he wrote to his aunt that he hoped the baby would be a boy
—when he was a student, jews were not permitted to sit in the
    front rows of lecture halls; he made it a point to
    stand through the lectures; ultimately, jews were
    allowed to sit
—he was a discus thrower
—according to some, he got along with everyone: jews, goyim,
    children
—he was caught a couple of times by the germans; they thought
    he was a polish smuggler
—once he was put on a train for treblinka; he jumped, was shot at
    and wounded, but got back to warsaw alive
—he believed in resistance

perspectives on the second world war

i

                it is a terror
in the closet   her knees
are limp   eyes straining to see
every object glows with a
private halo   pulling down
her skirt   the trickle
of urine along her thigh and calf
she wipes it carelessly with her hand
biting her lips she fixates on
pebbles and rusty nails along
the path to the truck   it is an oblivion
seen in matter-of-fact gestures
wiping the child's nose with her fingers
she says   blow   his eyes shine   as she
feels the pressure of the doorknob   palms
wet slipping out of her grasp   she whispers
not now   not yet   we've been so careful
he's a good child   just a little more time
she pleads with them   we will not be
careless anymore   this time the knob falls
into the glare of lights   voices scream
orders she does not understand   but obeys
blow   she tells him pulling down her skirt
and wiping his nose with her fingers   later
it is still over   has been over
since the knob slipped from her hand
like the wet fish that jumped while she tried
to scale it   later after the not yet
not now   the walk nude across the yard
she glimpses the meaning of the order

allows her eyes to widen for one
moment and see the path   it is a coldness
never before felt or imagined   she clutches
her hands tearing at her thighs   wailing
to the others she tries to lean on them
to explain the mistake   the small error
nothing is irrevocable   she screams   nothing
to them trying to lean   they push her away
and her hands cup the knob   for a better hold
to keep out the light   her world is cement
stone   iron

ii

listening to conversations   over brandy
i am always amazed at their certainty
about the past   how it could have been
different   could have been   turned around
with what ease   they transport themselves
to another time/place   taking the comfort
confidence of an after-dinner drink

                it would be too impolite
of me to say   my mother hid with me
for two years among ignorant peasants   who
would have turned us in   almost at once   had
they known who we were   who would have watched
with glee while we were carted off   even though
grandad had bounced me on his knees and fed me
from his own spoon   and my mother is a frightened
woman

                it would be too impolite
to say   you do not know yourselves   you do not know
others

II

conditions

i will take you   with me
next week   only if: you're
relaxed   and easy   and if:
you don't make   any trouble

if: you make any   and i mean   any
kind of trouble   i will leave you
here   with the two cats   a bowl
of water   and some   cookies

and i will be having   good times
without you   free without you
having nice times   not wishing
you were there   hanging on

and if: you choose to come
along   but spoil   my good times
and do not smile   and laugh
when it's appropriate

i will come   back without you
leave you there   among strangers
while i return   to the cats
and continue to feed them   regularly

and i will not acknowledge   any
postcards   telegrams   i will only say
you are out   or address unknown
or   you could be anywhere   by now

so let me repeat   and i do not make
idle threats   if: you want to stick
with me   and if: you want to go   and
want to come   with me   back and forth
smoothly easily   you can   if: you do every
thing exactly   precisely   as i want

periods of stress

it is unwise during periods of stress
or change to formulate new theories
case in point: when about to begin
a new love affair   without having ended
the previous one   do not maintain
that more freedom is required for the full expression
of individual personality   or that various
lifestyles are possible   and all kinds of interesting
situations   still need to be explored.

try instead: i am tired   tired
of the nearness   this small apartment
of the watering can and level of the window
shade.   i prefer to drift towards more spacious rooms
towards intimate restaurants and dimly lit unfamiliar
beds   new love techniques.   but
do not throw me out.   i am too
frightened to venture out alone.
let me stay till i'm secure again
somewhere else   and then leave me alone.

please don't touch me

please don't touch me
wait a moment
just wait one moment
until i'm not so cold

    the spider
    with its eyes
    into my insides
    the third eye
    warm with summer
    full of light
    now shrivelled
    atrophied
    dead to light

please don't touch me
wait a moment
just wait one moment
until i'm not so cold

    the spider
    with its eyes
    awake with me
    spread out
    behind my head
    silent still
    crawling away
    with the light

please don't touch me
wait a moment
just wait one moment
until i'm not so cold

the cracks
ceiling torn
caves of hollow
if breath is strong
silent still
motionless
breathless
airless
lightless
silent still
the balance
in control

please don't touch me
just wait a moment
just wait one moment
until i'm not so cold

dinosaurs and larger issues

for rachel

i

1. & 2.   the first two nights
she lay   diagonally across
the bed   clutching at the blankets
she refused me   room & warmth

3.   the third night
she told me   i can't handle
this   i can't handle   it
i slept   in the living room

4.   the fourth night
she said   this has to be
the last night   & moved
close to me

5.   the fifth night
she did not speak   about
it.

ii

they're never as big as i imagine
rachel informs me   whenever i enter
the reptile house   expecting cobras
to be jammed   wedged   bursting out of
into   every corner of the cage   muscles
tensing   i am always disappointed
with their slenderness   their comfort
and ease   as they relax   draping casually
over plastic trees

whales   she is earnest   should
be as big as ocean liners   instead
they swim content   in aquariums
trained to jump and leap   and it's true
they're large   but not like
they're supposed to be

rachel's eyes   narrow and widen
i do not reveal   some dinosaurs
full grown   were no bigger
than hens   that she could have
roasted   and served them
for dinner   with no fear of
leftovers

iii

in the dark   her features
are distinct   her skin white
translucent.   i see outlines
of bones.   she is crystal
my fingers   feel the thinness
of the flesh.   her mouth
is hard   demanding.   she
keeps her head turned away.
she does not look   directly
at me   except to brush away
the hair from my face   before
her tongue penetrates my mouth
then her eyes close quickly.
i study the hand's gesture
try to give it meaning.

in the dark   her features
are strong.   she lies relaxed
ready to accept   the touch
of my tongue   ready to be cupped
sucked into me   later she says
i cannot reciprocate.

iv

no i don't enjoy this
she says   biting my hand.
her mouth   which holds
endless kisses will never
say yes to me   just the hand
across my back   like a heavy hammer
or a quick furtive kiss
on the back of my neck
tell me   perhaps yes.

i just don't like cunts
she says   i don't like
them   she says to me.

v

i am sorry if i've made
you unhappy   i told her
sitting   at the furthest end
of the couch
                don't make
yourself so important
she answered   with confidence
there are larger issues
at stake.

vi

it's not the kind of person
you are   i try to explain to her
you have the power   to lift
your hand   to touch me as i pass
or to walk towards me   and hold
my face   so it's not the kind
of person   you are.

vii

at night   the vestiges
of other ages   influence
us.   there are
the sucking sounds   of your mouth
with mine   the moans of an ancient language
i easily recognize   my tongue
urging you on   slowly   deep
beneath the sea   or in some secret
cave   our nails: clawed we hold
each other   you and i
released from an unexpected
danger. exhausted we lick
each other's wounds   inflict
new ones   sharply.   our voices
echo   through the cave
return   and clash   on hard rock.
we know our bodies   and do not mind
them/ourselves   losing all sense
of proportions   limits.   we are equal
here   you and i.

afterwards   in the fire's flames
we see   cumbersome dinosaurs
rubbing their necks   against
each other   making small   sweet noises
tame and huge   so much larger than we dared imagine.

when the heart fails

when the heart fails   and over
fills with disappointment   rake
leaves   in the backyard;

gather them   in large green bags
stamp down   to make more room
gather more   and keep from the wind;

tie carefully with wire   to prevent
spillage   and going over the same ground;
since burning is forbidden   load up the car.

at the landfill   the gulls mill
and gawk   waiting.   this trip
will not please them.   there is nothing to eat.

it was good

for sharon

it was good:
the plant by your bed
green with sunlight
while we made love   your face
melted into marble
delicate pink   liquid
with desire   and later
walking through
haphazard streets
the sky empty
my arm through yours
the shrubbery   holding back
its spring greenness   your despondency
the cruising police   to remember
the slits in the blinds
the striped sun across
your face   the plant
the wetness of your mouth

flesh is cold

flesh is cold   and the bitch
moves too much in bed   crossing
and recrossing   unable to make
a warm spot and hold it   her skin
curls with the cold   shrivels
reduces her face to straight lines.
i wonder at the angle
of her back   solid in my face
she moves again   pretending
i am not there   till i pin her down
screaming   i am here   and you are not
here   alone

they're always curious

they're always curious about what you eat as if you were
some strange breed still unclassified by darwin & whether
you cook every night & wouldn't it be easier for you to
buy frozen dinners but i am quick to point out that my intra-
venous tubing has been taken out & they back up saying *i*
could never just cook for one person but i tell them it's
the same exactly the same as for two   except half

but more they're curious about what you do when the urge
is on & if you use a coke bottle or some psychedelic dildo
or electric vibrator or just the good old finger or whole
hand & do you mannipppppulllaaatttte yourself into a clit
orgasm or just kind of keep digging away at yourself & if
you mind it & when you have affairs doesn't it hurt when it's
over & it certainly must be lonely to go back to the old finger

& they always cluck over the amount of space you require
& certainly the extra bedroom seems unnecessary & i try to
explain that i like to move around & that i get antsy when
i have the urge so that it's nice to have an extra place
to go to when you're lonely & after all it seems small compen-
sation for using the good old finger & they're surprised be-
cause they never thought of it that way & it does seem reason-
able come to think of it

& they kind of probe about your future & if you have a will or
why you bother to accumulate all that stuff or what you plan
to do with your old age & aren't you scared about being put
away somewhere or found on your bathroom floor dead after
your downstairs neighbor has smelled you out but then of course
you don't have the worry of who goes first though of course
you know couples live longer for they have something to live
for & i try to explain i live for myself even when in love but
it's a hard concept to explain when you feel lonely

they did not build wings for them

they did not build wings for them
the unmarried aunts;   instead they
crammed them into old maids' rooms
or placed them as nannies with
the younger children;   mostly they
ate in the kitchen, but sometimes
were permitted to dine with the family
for which they were grateful and
smiled graciously as the food was passed.
they would eat slowly never filling
their plates and their hearts would
sink at the evening's end when it was
time to retreat into an upstairs corner.

but there were some who did not smile
who never wished to be grafted on
to the bursting houses. these few remained
indifferent to the family gatherings
preferring the aloneness of their small rooms
which they decorated with odd objects
found on long walks.   they collected
bird feathers and skulls unafraid to clean
them to whiteness;   stones which resembled
humped bears or the more common tiger and
wolf;   dried leaves whose brilliant colors
never faded; pieces of wood still covered
with fresh moss and earth which retained
their moisture and continued flourishing.
these they placed by their dresser mirrors
in arrangements reminiscent of secret rites
or hung over delicate watercolors of unruly
trees whose branches were about to snap
with the wind.

it happened sometimes that among these
one would venture even further.   periodically
would be heard vague tales of a woman
withdrawn and inaccessible suddenly disappearing
one autumn night leaving her room bare
of herself. women gossiped about a man.
but eventually word would come back
she had moved north to the ocean and lived
alone.   she was still collecting
but now her house was filled with crab
and lobster shells;   discolored claws
which looked like grinning south american
parrots trapped in fish nets decorated
the walls;   skulls of unidentifiable
creatures were arranged in geometric patterns
and soft reeds in tall green bottles
lined the windowsills.   one room
in the back with totally bare walls
was a workshop. here she sorted colored
shells and pasted them on wooden boards
in the shape of common flowers.   these she sold
without sentiment.

such a one might also disappear inland.
rumor would claim she had traveled in
men's clothing. two years later it would
be reported she had settled in the woods
on some cleared land.   she ran a small farm
mainly for supplying herself with food
and wore strangely patched dresses and shawls
of oddly matched materials.   but aloneness
was her real distinction.   the house was neat
and the pantry full   seascapes and pastoral
scenes hung on the walls.   the garden was
well kept and the flower beds clearly defined
by color: red   yellow   blue.   in the woods
five miles from the house she had an orchard.
here she secretly grafted and crossed varieties
creating singular fruit of shades and scents
never thought possible.   her experiments rarely
failed   and each spring she waited eagerly to see
what new forms would hang from the trees.
here the world was a passionate place and she
would visit it at night baring her breasts
to the moon.

the fish

for esther hyneman

directionless   it scavenged
never mapping   its own territory
or claiming   feeding rights.
it produced   spawning unfeelingly
generations unaware   of their origins
remaining indifferent   to them/it   all life
except   as it provided food   in dark shadows.

        there was no pattern   but
the broad cycle   and that also seemed
hidden from its consciousness   the irrevocable
past   present   future   so it was taken
by surprise   when suddenly it began to weaken
as the dryness entered its mouth   for it too
did not want to die   alone.

it lies half   eaten   brown burnt
covered in part by sand   the mouth
agonized   almost accusatory
it would be inhuman   to disturb its pain
washed inland   it sinks and drowns.

III

in between

it is always then
you notice   your lack
of brilliance   grace

feeling like a dying star
in the ram's horn
the fish's eye

that readies for a mute
explosion   noticed only
when its dark absence

startles a distracted astronomer.

the house

i

arranging it is far easier
than living it.   the books
stand ready on the shelves.

classifications by time or place
come naturally to me.   alone
finding the book important is difficult.

i've started to live here many mornings
opening my eyes vowing *this* morning
i will really begin.   objects intrude themselves:

floors need sweeping and one carton
unopened   is hidden in a closet.

ii

the telescope is still
disassembled   (at night
the skies are clear).

mirrors and lenses
lie in velvet lined cases.
i am afraid to use them.

iii

one of my cats was badly
clawed   i could see layers
of muscle and fat. my neighbor
warns there are foxes here.

i do not tell my neighbor
his cats look wild. i do not
know my neighbor's name.

iv

there are fears to which
i do not admit.   there are fears
which i refuse to name.   alone

in the dark   i am
afraid of others   but also
of the clean smell

of the refrigerator;
the freshness of chlorine
draws me.   i walk quickly
towards the bedroom.

v

this morning   i cleaned
the yard. i saw a face
from the city   in the trees.

the face was a mask
and i pulled it off
but there was nothing.

vi

patterns in rock originated from
pressure.   the veins were once separate
stones   pushed together   stamped into
other hard flesh.   they merged
and became ornamental.

                              the colors
blend surprisingly well.   rings
match shapes and textures.   unwilling
inanimate   they played their roles
the iceberg scraping off layers   till
the desired smoothness was achieved.

vii

i do not understand my place
in it.   it seems to have a life
of its own   made by others
simply on loan   for a year.

they ask me: how is
your book?   and i give accurate
gas meter readings   wondering
where i will be next year.

the world here is fluid
the beaches undefined.   there are rocks
whose function   i do not know.

blending

in montauk it gets so clear   that sky and sea
become discrete like   jigsaw pieces you can pull
apart   and fling yourself through the space
between.   it is a constant temptation   for here
is neither love nor admiration.   you get on
on your own   or you don't get on.   it's a cold
world   each part unto itself: dune   rock   tree
defined without mirrors or likenesses.   here nothing
borrows from anything else   but is entirely itself.

> *—in a motel on 27*
> *he turned me to the wall   pushed my knees up into*
> *a fetal position   and then came in me   from the back*
> *saying   ooooooh yes   ooooooh yes   as if he'd just*
> *conquered me and given me warning.   and he touched me*
> *nowhere   so I stared at the grimy white wall of the*
> *room   at the thin streak of blood from the cat whose*
> *tail had been amputated the week before   while he kept*
> *saying ooooooooooh yes   and i remembered the question:*
> *didn't i mind who the father was?   but the blood came*
> *as usual.*

in montauk birds are fat   as if feeding on flowering
flesh.   they move through the indifferent landscape
like gluttons.   blue jays screech perpetually   but
the other species survive without effort.   and always
the seagulls remain sleek and proudbellied feasting
at the landfill   and growing worldly from motel garbage.
they've learned to ignore the obvious: alien rocks
dragged here by glaciers.   they soar and circle and descend
and sleep   only to wake   and eat.

edges

1/

the only reason she was not able to make it on her own
though she'd been on her own and alone most of her life
was that she'd never before been forced to distinguish
herself from trees   or sand and sea.   and it became ob-
vious that when it came to rocks   she could never prove
her own distinctness.   the realization   occurring one
very clear   transparent day   when she could see all the
way to the end of the point   frightened her so much   she
ran back to the house and rolled herself up in a blanket.
first   she closed the bathroom door.

2/

the preoccupation with plants   constant watering and hover-
ing over them   checking the buds and fingering the leaves
was another major symptom.   she did not want to admit it
to herself immediately.   she continued watching them some-
times stealthily   hoping she would catch even the minutest
movement.   (she turned the plants away from the sun   and
they turned back.)   it was impossible to catch   to seize
their breath.   she would pretend that when she watered them
the leaves trembled.   but that was fantasy.

3/

though she did not want to mouth it   she knew the words
were missing.   somewhere she'd lost the vocabulary   per-
haps the black night when she pushed herself outside and
down the road   though her hands continued gesticulating
when she ran towards the ocean.   it was a loss she did
not regret   finding it was better to listen   then to manu-
facture.

4/

she could not tell if this was birth or death   moving
out of   or into the grave.   the sand was alternately
hot and dry   and cold and wet   too extreme in either
case   and the ocean took on a different feeling each day
without warning.   in the winter the dune shrubbery seemed
to hold its breath.   she watched it keenly   her eyes
lowered   away from the horizon.

5/

she had kept the seedlings in the bedroom   but that had
become a terrible burden.   she found it impossible to
concentrate and so moved them into the kitchen.   the bed-
room door would remain closed at all times   day or night.
she lived alone   but feared intrusions she could not arti-
culate.   it was not human contact   or human harm.   ra-
ther it was   the kitchen   its smell of food which frightened
her.   it was undefined   and she desperately needed strict
outlines   an unfilled space demarcated.   She chose the bed-
room   keeping the door closed   day and night.

6/

whenever the phone rang she was startled   not because she
didn't expect anyone to call   but because it seemed that here
surrounded by sand   and smell of salt and cooking meat   the
ring was inappropriate.   it was as if some strange creature
had made a demanding noise   insisted on recognition which she
was unwilling to give.   she never knew how to speak   or what
to say.

7/

crushing time between waking and sleeping was a daily con-
cern.   she moved slowly hoping it would move past   post-
poning the waking moment till almost stupor.   it was all
limitless.   seeing the beach fade into the fog   she'd
turn suddenly and discover her footprints had already been
covered by the wind.   no trace at all   as if she'd been
born on that spot in that moment.   she was amazed how
easily markings disappeared and became a part of the shore.
the bluffs stood coldly   eroding.

8/

there had been that moment looking down towards the point
when the horizon had distinctly separated the ocean and sky
and waves came in regular motions   building and collapsing
in unending fury   that she felt herself losing ground   eva-
porating.   she tried to think of a small pale blue flower
which had appeared the day before.   but it was drowned in
the foam which ran towards her toes like soapsuds.   the
water receded   taking the flower with it   and she watched
as she was pushed inland   and the wet sand was pulled away
from her until she felt in one moment it would be too late
and ran back to the house   and rolled herself up in a blank-
et.

9/

the pale blue flower was a surprise.   the plant seemed to
be only leaves   she had stared at it for a long time try-
ing to remember a word   brack   or bracti   she could not re-
call exactly a lesson she'd once heard.   she was frighten-
ed again.   all this breath   she thought.   she considered
withholding water   that was for a fraction of a second   and
then watered it immediately.   supper had to be cooked.
she checked the bedroom door.

10/

she knew of course that here it would have to be serious
because no one would look in or call   for days   so it was
a serious decision to be weighed carefully   and when fully
sober.   she continued collecting rocks   arranging them on
the deck   planting new seeds   and feeling the scratching
as imperceptible as a forgotten dream   down at the base of
her skull.   she continued cooking   and freezing the food
and answering the phone when it rang   and trying to remember
old words she once knew: viscera   stasis   inchoate.

11/

there was no saving here and no one to advise her and she
really did not want to listen except whether it was acidic
or alkaline   and whether sun was necessary or humidity   or
if repotting might be helpful for growth   or if fertilizer
had to be used.   she kept taking books out of the library
renewing them   but it was hard to hold it all in.

it culminated in a rage she could not contain.   the door had
not been closed properly   and was pushed open by the draft
from the kitchen   the curtains moved as if breathing in and
out against the screen.   she knew it was too late   and she
could not control it anymore.   she walked to the beach and
scooped up the foam rubbing it against her face.   she squeezed
slimy seaweed   till it squirted strange juices   that trickled
down her legs like green semen.   she walked for a mile collect-
ing all the fish skulls she could find   and arranged them in
concentric circles   placing a rock in the middle.   finally
she carried some large stones to the foot of a bluff   hoping
to prevent erosion.

IV

aesthetic distance

only it
can help in the arrangement

: a child   fat
ordinary   except
for its flabbiness
    except
for the bullet hole
through its belly

: a discolored puncture

: a mother (or grandmother
leathered   hard
staring
beyond the bullet hole
beyond the belly

into a dry   brown
hard part of this earth

self-dialogues

i

it seems that you and i
have not talked
now   for a long time
and today   walking by
the gardens   i first noticed
how trees have their own
diseases   cancerous-
like growths that choke their trunks.

                    once
when i saw a tree cut in half
i said in surprise
it is wet
and you said back:
it is a living thing
and we tend to forget
that like blood
this transparent
dew   leaks life.

i'd forgotten your existence
your heavy boredom in winter
the wetness of life   sitting
here   staring at the incomplete
dry wooden bookshelves   waiting
to be trimmed   sanded
smoothed down from original irregularities
how trees have their own
diseases   that wound
and suffocate with sawdust
their rigid arteries.

ii

today   the day
had no beginning
in the afternoon
i took a walk on the esplanade
and stared at the river.

water is a rare sight
in the city.   you have to search
for it   through secret side streets
of elegant neighborhoods
or abandoned factory areas
with punctured windows.   glass
remains a deterrent

                    but it can
be reached   and from a certain
height   retains a quality
of purity freshness   though
perhaps it is too tame
too calm today   to reflect its
ocean origins.

iii

it is not a question
of belonging   but rather
of finding a place
and you   are difficult
to place.

the decor of the apartment
has been set   i've worked
hard for the final effect
the position of planters
the colors of the prints
the wall rugs   a feeling
of easy life   with the darker
tones of understanding.

                              frankly
i don't want to disturb
the current scheme   and it is
inconvenient   to say the least
of you to come now   at this time
when i had it all so well arranged
insisting   with your monotony
on the pain.

                         yes yes
pain is a part of life
but i'd prefer
you kept yours
to yourself.

iv

i've recognized you
in the terror-worn
faces of old women
pigeon feeders   who
carry frayed social security
checks   and politely belch
their acid-eaten stomachs
behind their hands.

i've seen you
in the words
of their forced conversations
with young cashier girls
all pink in their
striped uniforms
young girls
who smile   pity
in embarrassment.

i remember how you
used to stand
putting on lipstick.
they also preen
and watch the color run in the cracks
of their skin   and
smear into a wound.
how coquettishly
they prepare
for street society
for passersby   pulling
down their skirts
over their tired bodies
saying: well someone
will see   and it is always good
to look nice.

i've never liked looking
at them   though i've
stared in pained fascination
thinking of you.

v

i would never have placed
you here   but rather in
some cardboard room   a meager
supply of food in the refrigerator.

and yet i've been lonely
of late   and would not mind
some company   just to fill up
the space.   the living room
is lovely this afternoon
light with sun;
some plants are already
beginning to bloom   and
perhaps it might cheer you
to take in the warmth   of the colors
here

i would not mind
such company
that drank in the brightness
and felt my efforts
nourishing.

vi

last night i dreamt i was
a gaunt   and lifeless tree
and you climbed into me to nest.
you were calm   so serious
as you wrapped your legs
around my trunk   and pressed
your body against me.   and
wherever your human skin
touched my rough bark   i
sprouted branches   till
lush with leaves i grew
all green and silver   frail
like tinsel   holding you
asleep   in my wooden arms.

Two Sisters:
Helen and Eva Hesse

(1978)

An Introduction

The two sisters were born in Hamburg, Germany: Helen in 1933 and
Eva in 1936. In 1938, their parents placed them on a children's train to
Holland, to safety, to an aunt and uncle who never came to pick them up
in Amsterdam. So the girls were sent to a Catholic children's home, safe in
Holland, Catholic, out of Germany. But Eva became sick, was taken to a
hospital, alone away from Helen, and Helen stayed in the home with the
rest of the children, alone away from Eva. After a few months, their parents
arrived and the Hesse family was reunited.

In 1939, the Hesses emigrated to safety, to the United States. During the
next few years, the parents separated, divorced, found other partners. The
girls lived with their father and his new wife (whose name was also Eva),
went to school. Six years after their arrival, their mother sought safety again,
committed suicide in January of 1945. From then on, her daughter Eva
feared January.

The two sisters grew up, got married. Eva was an artist, married, became
known, divorced. Her father became ill, had to be cared for and watched
for many years. He died in 1966. And then Eva became sick, went to the
hospital, found she had a brain tumor, cancer. She died at the age of thirty-
three on May 29, 1970.

"Two Sisters" is a monologue by Helen Hesse, surviving older sister of
the artist Eva Hesse and sole surviving member of the Hesse family.

Two Sisters: A Monologue

I.

Her nightmares were always worse
though I remember more of what
actually happened: the nuns polite
indifferent   the marble floors
my knees   white with numbness
from kneeling too long.
She dreamt of black pockets of space
starless voids through which she'd float alone
nothing to touch   nothing to be touched by.
Then she'd wake   and scream into the night
and Papa would come   to tighten the covers.
He'd whisper: "You're perfectly safe now.
Hush.   I've tied you down."

Her screams would
cut off my dreams   of the goodbye kiss
the brush of skin
against skin
in heavy damp air
how Mamma wiped tears from her dark deep eyes
then straightened the fur piece   around her collar
and   how Papa pinned our names to our coats
telling us softly: "Be strong, be proud."
And then   I'd watch them again and again
standing and waving   their handkerchiefs high
till they were so small   just bits of mud
on the splattered glass.

II.

There are times   when the heart
like a young   and inexperienced
ancient queen   sick and over-
burdened by nightly dreams   begins
to harden   to close in upon herself;
nor does she find ease   or safety
in the words of the sorcerers
astronomers   in the scheming court.
Instead   determined   she watches
learns in silence   that all times
are times of crises
that throughout her lifetime
there will be no peace
that again   and again   her realm
will be besieged by warring tribes
with alien   unpredictable ways.
And so   she tightens the borders
around her unhappy realm   and rules.

             The heart   too
when unprepared for the world and its rude ways
mistakenly learns   to exclude pain and pleasure
alike   hoping to achieve serenity.

III.

Take, for example, the children:
She simply did not understand   about them
that they were not pieces
whose internal wiring   could be bent
and twisted out of an unnamed need
or discarded when they resisted imagined forms.
They were not art.
Whenever she'd visit   she'd sit and watch
as hand in hand   they'd choreograph
maneuvers   on their blazing boards
bend with the curves of the hill
like birds I've seen   perhaps imagined.
She'd look astonished   and she'd laugh:
"You've forged the great American dream."
Then she'd turn and think about something else.

In Europe   life was less distinct:
more room — no — a tendency towards shadows
within the ancient   stone yards.
The beggars   begged among the poor
calling to the shuttered windows
their monotonous   call.
It was — not a gloom exactly —
but an earnestness   a realization
of the seriousness of things.   And Eva,
she, I think, felt safer with those daytime shadows
more at ease with light   transformed and stretched
by obstructing walls   into a narrowing darkness.

It was quite simple: I preferred the sun.

IV.

Europe was history and sepia: photographs frayed
at the edges   sometimes torn or folded
thick postcards   slashed the face scarred
the body stiff and awkward.   With luck
you'd see the eyes   wide
a sense of life   of attitude: the cap
in hand   slicked down hair   buttoned shoes.
But always   they remained   an earthly brown
and with age   the light around them brightened
and the figures would bow into a faded background.

Our albums   are so different
harsh with colors   seen
only   on clear and sunny days
on empty beaches
water reflecting light   of sun and sky
are such colors ever seen.   Yet in our albums
they glow   in every season   in any place
bright and sharp   such health and freshness
in the midst   of foul urban air
or war   or sickness: such health and freshness
in our photographs.

V.

She'd never leave   old wounds alone.
I'd   reason with her   to get more control
but she'd press her lips   and say: "Let's face it
we're just not the same."   And turn her back
as if—it's hard to say what she really wanted.

Once   I remember she said to me:
"You're like a fortress
I once dreamed of: all mortar   stone
and iron.   I scaled its walls   with bare
hands and feet   tearing myself on the crude
exterior.   Eventually   I reached the top
gained access to its rooms and halls.

Inside: it was quite empty.   Helen   it
protected nothing."
                              She had a way
of hurting deeply   then pulling back.
She'd begin to cry
then touch me   with such ease
hold my face   between her hands.
She'd sob and weep
in a rush of ecstatic love:
"Helen, forgive me.   You know how I am."

I've never felt that free.

VI.

I'd sometimes visit her in New York
and stare across the river at the Jersey shore.
I'd try to see it   through her eyes.
"Dead," she'd say   without a second thought.

Her art was everything.
She never understood   that I needed
ground   a place to root myself
to tie myself down
that I could not float   like she did
never knowing what strange   new thing
would burst from me   demanding of attention.
She'd cry: "You're lucky, you've escaped
the terrors."   I'd bite hard and reply:
"I've fought to keep them out."

VII.

I read statistics about this place
Yet I feel safe.   The children are strong.
He's always with me.   I'm not alone.

Perhaps that's weak.   I think
she did not have to be   the way she was.
I've survived   just by my own will.
She died of illness.   Yet the critics are sure:
she wouldn't have lived longer   anyway.
Young death is suicide   no matter what.

I still see her   so so clearly:
how she turned   bewildered
frightened   already ill.
"Helen," she said, "I've just begun
to understand it all.   Why now?   Is it my fault?
Must it end badly   botched up   like it began?"

Sometimes at night I circle the room
like an angry tiger around its prey:
genes   environment   our own will.
But I'm no expert on these things.
Resistance's elusive.   The children complain
that I am too hard.
I feel jealous of him   when one of them cries.
But I'm afraid   I want them to know
how easily these battles   are lost.
I want them to know —
and then I think:
        Eva, sister — what dreams we both had.

Keeper of Accounts

(1982)

I

....

FROM THE MONKEY HOUSE AND OTHER CAGES

The voices are those of female monkeys born and raised in a zoo.

Monkey 1

/1/

from the beginning
she was always dry   though
she'd press me close
prying open my lips:

the water warm
the fruit   sour   brown
apples bruised and soft.

hungry for dark   i'd sit
and wait   devour dreams
of plain sun and sky
large leaves   trunks   dark
and wet with sweet thick sap.

                    but morning
brought back the space
and cement   her weakened
body   my head against her
breast: my mouth empty.

/2/

yet she was   all
my comfort: her sharp
ribs against my cheek
her bony fingers   rough
in fluffing me dry.

she showed me   all
the space   the changing
colors outside   then

pulled me back   forced
me to sit with her
in a shadowy corner.

on certain clear days
she'd shrug   hold me in the sun:
her fur lacked smoothness
her body warmth.

/3/

in the midst of heat
they took me   with smooth
round strokes   and hushing
sounds.
          she sat silent
at first   sniffing their sweat
their stale breath   then leaped on one
her eyes wide   her claws poised and sharp.
          he grunted   deep
from within   an empty cavern
echoing the storm outside
flicked her off   and dragged me out.

i could hear her sound
as if a sea lion roared
then becoming tired
                    drowned.

/4/

their space was smaller
cramped and low   the air
foul   with their sweat
their salt.
       and their motions
were sharp   as they spread me out
clamped me down
for the opening probe.

          i did not move
just sucked my breath
with each new venture   into my deepest parts
and then   with time
i became   a dark dull color
a gray rain   blending
with the liquid   of her eyes.

/5/

when they returned me
the air was ice:
bare branches   meshed
against a hard   dark sky.

i sat alone.   we were
separate now   though
she was still there
in the space   next to mine.
her fur was stiff   her nostrils spread
she eyed me   circled
her back arched   ready for attack.

later   as the food was dropped
she leaped forward
hissed   snatched bits of fruit
from my side   of the bars.

/6/

a day   and a day
the pools   dead and dry
i'd sit and stare
into the cold   into the empty trees.

but she seemed   at rest
pressing against the bars
eyes closed   alone   on the other side.
only when i ate   she'd look sharp at me
her mouth moving
as i swallowed   each bite

and as night blackened us
she'd gather her scraps
enclose herself   in her arms.

/7/

the male   sleek-furred
was young   and active
when they forced him through to me.

i stayed in place   all
eyes and ready   while she leaped
in frenzy   retreated to the furthest wall.
he kept his distance
ignoring her   ignoring me
ate small morsels   tumbled
stared outside.

the ice was thawing
the pools filled and quiet.
i listened   as the soil
sopped   became mud
deep   and brown.

/8/

soon the trees budded   and i
pinked   softened   and presented.
he penetrated   withdrew
penetrated   withdrew
over   and over
till i was dry
and hard.
                    she sat
relaxed and quiet
began to chew apples
slowly picking out
each black seed.

/9/

                    later
i cramped   shriveled
then opened   wide   wide
my flesh thin and stretched
till: it burst forth
a thing   so strange
so pale   and hairless
a mass of flesh   separate from mine.

and through the heat
and heavy trees   the sound of water
the light of the moving sun:
the male ate regularly
the small one sucked
i mashed the sour fruit
between my lips.

she watched us all
as we would swallow
hoard   any piece of rind
or seed   that she could find.

/10/

the male was taken:
i turned my back.
the small one was taken:
i was held to one side.

and again   and again
the trees emptied again
the soil became hard
then became soft again.

and the cage is   all
mine   and i have myself:
touching my fur
pulling my face

while she moves so slowly
without any sound
eating   pacing
twisting her arms   around the hard bars.

/11/

sometimes at night   i watch
her asleep: the rigid bones
the thinned out fur

and i can see clearly
the sky   the bars
as we sat together
in a spot of sun
and she   eyes closed
moved me
moved me
to the sound of the waters
lapping
in the small   stone pools
outside.

Monkey 2

/1/

to state each horror
would be redundant.   the objects
themselves suffice: a broken comb
an umbrella handle   a piece of blue
plastic   chipped pocket mirror.

the face is unfriendly.
i try to outstare it   but
it persists   moving

spastically   the eyes
twitching   open   shut
nose quivering   wrinkled fingers
picking at the ears.   i do not know

this stranger.

/2/

i have heard of tortures
yet remain
strangely safe.

       but at night
i am torn by my own
dreams   see myself live
the grossest indignities   probes

and unable to rip myself from my flesh
i remain silent   not
uttering sound   nor moan   not
bothering to feel pain.

waking   in early light
alone   untouched
i cry over my safety.

/3/

when they first come
they screech with wildness
flinging themselves against the wall
and then against the bars.

some sit and cry for days
some   never recover and
die.
        they are familiar
yet crap uncontrollably   plead
shiver and rock.   i refuse

to have anything to do with them
till they learn to behave.

/4/

at her arrival   she was
stunned and bruised.   she
folded up   refusing to eat

her mouth grim.   i staked
out my territory   recognizing
her fierceness   her strength.

but she weakened   grew sick
was removed without resistance
returned three days later
shaved patches on her arms.

later she told me: we create
the responses around us.

/5/

I remember the grasp of her claws
the vicious bite   the scar
still on my leg.   she was crazed

jabbering   then attacking
again.   and the sun seemed to fall away
into coldness   as i pressed myself
against the corner   the hardened sand
under my nails.   i began to gnaw
through concrete   my face raw.

they took her away
and when she came back
she did not look at me.

/6/

scatter yourself
i told her   moving
myself into the left
corner   where i sat
observing the movement
of her head.

                    she nodded
seemed to sleep
then stood up   pointing
outside.   the leaves were
red.   it was a falling time
noisy   dry twigs cracking
off nearby trees. i felt

content   watching myself
while she pointed   the leaves
red.

/7/

                    and finally
she said   this is enough
and began to bang her head
against the wall   one thud

after another thud   she batted
herself beginning to bleed
throwing herself and falling.

they came   and tried to seize
her   while the sun vanished
and the trees   moved slowly

and everyone   so still
afraid to breathe: the moon
all fresh   and the birds
small balls of feathers.

i puked as they dragged her out:
tufts of fur on the stone floor.

/8/

when she died   i mourned
a silent mourning.
                        and
the others asked
asked   asked
and poked at me.

there had been much between us
in gesture.   mostly i remember
her yellowed teeth   her attempt
at tameness.

/9/

there had been no sound:
just the motion of   our hands
our lips sucked in
toes pointed   outward.
it had been enough.

                      dizzy
with messages   i would lie
down   dream of different
enclosures.

II

DIFFERENT ENCLOSURES

Contexts

for Tillie Olsen

Dollars damn me.
HERMAN MELVILLE

I have no patience with this dreadful idea that whatever you have in
you has to come out, that you can't suppress true talent. People can
be destroyed; they can be bent, distorted, and completely crippled.
KATHERINE ANNE PORTER

I.

I am helping proofread the history
of a dead language. I read out loud
to an old man whose eyes have failed
him. He no longer sees the difference
between a period or a comma, a dash
or a hyphen, and needs me, for I under-
stand how important these distinctions are.

The room is crammed with books, books
he had systematically tagged for future
projects — now lost. Sounds pour out
of me. I try to inject some feeling
and focus, concentrate on the meaning
of each linguistic phrase. On the edge
of my vision, he huddles over a blurred
page, moves his magnifying glass from line
to line, and we progress. Time passes.
My voice is a stranger's, sensible and
calm, and I, the cornered, attentive hostess,
listen in silence as it conjectures the his-
tory of languages long dead without a trace.
How, I wonder, did I become what I am not?

I request a break. The sounds cease.
I check the clock, calculate, write
figures in a notebook. I am numb
and stiff, walk up and down the hall,
stare into busy offices. I wait.
I wait for something forgotten, something
caught and bruised: a brown feather,
a shaft of green light, a certain word.
I bend, drink water, remember stubborn
clams clinging to the muddy bottom.

II.

The building across the street
has an ordinary facade, a view of the park
and rows of symmetrical spotless windows.
Each morning, the working women come to perform
their duties. They are in starched white,
could pass for vigilant nurses keeping
order and quiet around those about to die.
And each morning, idle women
in pale blue housecoats, frilled and fluffed
at the edges, stare out of double windows,
waiting for something to begin.

With whom would you change places, I ask
myself, the maid or the mistress?

III.

The clock sucks me back. I calculate the loss,
return to the books, his unrecognizing eyes.
He is unaware of the pantomime outside,
feels no rage that I and the world are lost
to him, only mourns the words dead on the page.
We begin again. I point to the paragraph,
synchronize the movement of eye and mouth,
abandon all pretense of feeling. Silently I float
out, out towards the horizon, out towards the open sea,
leaving behind the dull drone of an efficient machine.

I am
there again, standing by the railing, watching
the whales in their narrow aquarium, watching
their gleaming grace in the monotonous circle, watching
how they hunger for fleshly contact, how the young keeper
places his human hand in their rough pink mouths,
rubs their tongues, splashes them like babies. I cannot
watch them enough, but feel deeply ashamed for I know
the price.

With a shock I realize we are not together,
that he is lost, caught in a trap.
He sounds the words over and over, moves
the glass back and forth, insists there is
a lapse in meaning. I sit silent, tense, watch
as he painfully untangles the subtle error, watch
as he leans back exhausted saying: "I knew something
was wrong! I knew from the context that something
was wrong!"

IV.

At the end of the day I stack the galleys,
mark an *x* where we've been forced to stop.
He is reluctant to let me go, anxious, un-
certain about the coming days, but I smile,
assure him they'll be all the same. Alone,
I rush for the bulb-lit train, for the empty
corner of the dingy car, then begin the struggle
against his vacant stare, against the memory
of the crowded shelves.

It is a story, I tell myself, at least
a story, that one Sunday when I refused
to go to work. Fifteen, bored with inventory
and weekend jobs, I stayed in bed and,
already expert, called in sick. Her rage
was almost savage, wild. She paced
through the apartment, returned to me again
and again saying *"Get up! Get up now!"*
as if I were in mortal danger. But nothing
would move me from my bed, from the sun
cutting through the iron fire escape outside,
from the half-finished book about the man
and the whale. "It's not that much money,"
I called to her.

And then her inexplicable silence. At first
she sat in the kitchen, fingering the piece
of cloth, staring absently at the teacup.
Finally, she got up, began pinning the pattern.
Soon I heard the clean sound of the scissors
against the kitchen table, then silence again
as she basted. Much later that day, she worked
on the machine, and still she did not speak
to me, just let the bobbing needle make its own
uninterrupted noise. And as I went to bed
new with the excitement of that sea of words,
filled with my own infinite possibilities, she
continued sewing, fulfilling her obligation
for the next day's fitting.

V.

The blind man balances easily in the rocking
car. He moves among us, sings, shakes a tin
cup. Most of us think it's all a con, but it
makes no difference. Pose is part of necessity.
Riding each evening through the echoing tunnels,
I've begun to believe in the existence of my own
soul, its frailty, its ability to grow narrow,
small. I've begun to understand what it means
to be born mute, to be born without hope of speech.

Work Sonnets

with Notes and a Monologue about a Dialogue

I: Work Sonnets

i.

iceberg
I dream   yearning
to be fluid.
through how many nights
must it float   cumbersome
for how many centuries
of sun   how many
thousands of years
must it wait
so that one morning
I'll wake
as water of lake
of ocean
of the drinking well?

and day breaks.

ii.

today was another day. first i typed some
letters that had to get out. then i spent
hours xeroxing page after page after page
till it seemed that i was part of the machine
or that it was a living thing like me. its
blinking lights   its opening mouth   looked
as if they belonged to some kind of terrible
unthinking beast to whom i would always be bound.
oblivious to my existence   it simply waited
for its due   waited for me to keep it going
waited for me to provide page after page after page.
when it overheated   i had to stop while it
readied itself to receive again. so i typed
some letters that had to get out. and he said

he was pleased with the way things were going.

iii.

today was my day for feeling bitter. the xerox
broke down completely   and the receptionist
put her foot down   and made it clear to the repairmen
that *we* couldn't afford to keep such a machine
and it was costing *us* extra money every time *we* had
to xerox outside. they hemmed and hawed and said
the fuzz from the carpet clogged things up   and
then they worked on it. and she watched over them
and made sure it was going properly when they left.
by then i'd fallen behind and he asked me to stay
late   and i said i was tired and really wanted to go
home. so he said it was really important and i could
come in late tomorrow with pay. so i said okay and
stayed. but i didn't feel any better about it.

a morning is not an evening.

iv.

volcano
I dream   yearning
to explode.
for how many centuries
of earth   relentless
grinding   how many
thousands of unchanged
years   buried
will it take
so that one morning
I'll wake as unfettered flame
as liquid rock
as fertile ash?

and day breaks.

v.

today was my day for taking things in stride.
i was helpful to the temp in the office next
door   who seemed bewildered and who had definitely
lied about her skills. the dictaphone was
a mystery to her and she did not know how to use
the self-erasing IBM nor the special squeezer
to squeeze in the words. she was the artist type:
hair all over the place   and dirty fingernails.
i explained everything to her   during her coffee
break   when she had deep creases in her forehead.
i felt on top of things. during lunch
i went out and walked around window shopping
feeling nice in the afternoon sun. and then
i returned and crashed through a whole bunch

of letters so i wouldn't have to stay late.

vi.

today was my day for feeling envy. i envied
every person who did not have to do what i
had to do. i envied every person who was rich
or even had 25 cents more than me   or worked
even one hour less. i envied every person who
had a different job   even though i didn't want
any of them either. i envied poor homeless children
wandering the streets because they were little
and didn't know the difference   or so i told myself.
and i envied the receptionist who'd been there
for years and years and years and is going to retire
soon   her hearing impaired from the headpiece she'd
once been forced to wear. for her it was over.
she was getting out. i envied her so much today.

i wanted to be old.

vii.

rock
I dream   yearning
to yield.
how many centuries
of water pounding
for how many thousands
of years   will it take
to erode this hardness
so that one morning
I'll wake
as soil
as moist clay
as pleasure sand
along the ocean's edge?

and day breaks.

viii.

today we had a party. he said he had gotten a
new title and brought in a bottle of wine during
lunch and we all sat around and joked about how
we'd become such important people and drank the
wine. and the receptionist got a little giddy
and they told her to watch it or she would develop
a terrible reputation which was not appropriate for
someone her age and maturity. and she laughed and
said "that's all right. i'll risk it." and the temp
from the office next door came in to ask me to go to
lunch. so we gave her some wine and she said she'd
been hired permanently and was real happy because
she'd been strung out and getting pretty desperate.
i noticed her hair was tied back and her nails neater.

and then we all got high and he said to everyone
this was a hell of a place. and then he announced
he had a surprise for me. he said he was going to
get a new xerox because it was a waste of my time to
be doing that kind of work and he had more important
things for me to do. and everyone applauded and the
receptionist said she hoped this one was better than
the last because we sure were losing money on that
old clinker. and he assured her it was. and then he
welcomed the temp to the floor and said "welcome aboard."
and he told her across the hall they treat their people
like we treat our people and their place is one hell
of a place to work in as she'd soon discover. and then
he winked over in my direction and said: "ask her.

she knows all about it."

ix.

dust
I dream   yearning
to form.
through how much emptiness
must it speed
for how many centuries
of aimless orbits
how many thousands
of light years   must it wait
so that one morning
I'll wake
as cratered moon
as sea-drenched planet
as exploding sun?

and day breaks.

and day breaks.

II: Notes

Says she's been doing this for 12 years. Her fifth job since she started working at 18. The others were: office of paper box manufacturing company (cold and damp almost all year round); office of dress factory (was told she could also model for buyers; quit because buyers wanted to feel the materials and her; was refused a reference); real estate office; and this, which she considers the best one. Through high school, she worked part time contributing towards household expenses.

Extremely sharp with them. Says: "I'm not a tape recorder. Go through that list again." Or: "It's impossible. I've got too much to do." Two days ago, she told me: "Make them set *reasonable* priorities. Don't make yourself nuts. You're not a machine."

Am surprised, because I always feel intimidated. But she seems instinctively to understand power struggles. Is able to walk the fine line between doing her job well and not knocking herself out beyond what she thinks she is being paid for. And she *is* good. Quick. Extremely accurate. Am always embarrassed when they return things with errors and ask me to do them over again. Never happens to her. She's almost always letter perfect.

I've told her she should demand more. The dictaphone is old and the typewriter is always breaking down. She should make them get her better equipment. It's too frustrating the way it is. She shrugged. Said it really didn't matter to her. Was surprised at her indifference.

Friendly, yet somehow distant. Sometimes I think she's suspicious of me, though I've tried to play down my background. I've said to her: "What's the difference? We're doing exactly the same work, aren't we?" Did not respond. Yet, whenever I've had trouble, she's always been ready to help.

Her life: an enigma. Have no idea what preoccupies her. Would be interested in knowing her dreams. Hard for me to imagine. This is a real problem. First person demands such inside knowledge, seems really risky. Am unclear what the overall view would be. What kind of vision presented. How she sees the world. How she sees herself in it. It seems all so limited, so narrow. Third person opens it up. But it would be too distanced, I think. I want to be inside her. Make the reader feel what she feels. A real dilemma. I feel so outside.

Says she reads, but is never specific what. Likes music, dancing. Smokes. Parties a lot, I think, for she seems tired in the morning and frequently says she did not get much sleep. Lives by herself. Thinks she should get married, but somehow can't bring herself to do it. "I like having the place to myself," she said the other day. Didn't specify what she was protecting.

Attitude towards them remains also unformulated. Never theorizes or distances herself from her experience. She simply responds to the immediate situation. Won't hear of organizing which she considers irrelevant (and also foreign inspired). Yet she's very, very fair and helpful to others and always indignant if someone is being treated unfairly. Whenever a temp arrives, she always shows her what's what. Tells her not to knock herself out. Reminds her to take her coffee break. Once gave up her lunch hour so one of them could go to the dentist for a bad tooth. Did it without hesitation. For a stranger.

Q: Is she unique or representative? The final piece: an individual voice? or a collective one?

I've learned a lot here, I think. It hasn't been much of a loss as I expected. At least I've gotten some ideas and some material. But thank god I'm leaving next week. Can't imagine spending a whole life doing this.

III: A Monologue about a Dialogue

And she kept saying: "There's more. Believe me, there's more."

And I was kind of surprised because I couldn't imagine what more there could be. And then I began to wonder what she meant by the more, like maybe a bigger apartment or more expensive restaurants.

But she said that wasn't it, not really. "I'm not materialistic," she said and then looked kind of hopeless, as if I could never understand her. "I just want to *do* something," she said, obviously frustrated. And she looked hopeless again. And then she took a big breath, as if she was going to make a real effort at explaining it to me.

"It's just," she said, "it makes no difference whether I'm here or not. *Anyone* can do this. And I've always wanted to do special, important work."

Well, that made me laugh, because I've stopped wanting to do any work at all. All work is bullshit. Everyone knows that. No matter how many telephones and extensions, no matter how many secretaries, no matter how many names in the rolodex. It's all bullshit.

But she disagreed. "No," she said. "There's really important work to be done."

"Like what?" I asked curious, for I've seen enough of these types running around telling me how important it is to do this or that and just because they're telling me it's important they start feeling that they're important and doing important work. So I was curious to see what she'd come up with.

But she was kind of vague, and said something about telling the truth and saying things other people refused to say. And I confess I'd never heard it put that way before.

"I want to be able to say things, to use words," she explained.

"Oh, a writer," I said. I suddenly understood.

"Well, yes. But not like you think. Not romances or anything like that. I want to write about you and how you work and how it should be better for you."

"So that's it," I said, understanding now even more than I had realized at first. "So that's the important work. That certainly sounds good. Good for you, that is. But what about me? Do you think there's more for me? Because I'm not about to become a writer. And I don't know why I should just keep doing this so you have something to write about that's important. So can you think of something more for me? I mean I can't do anything except this."

And I could feel myself getting really mad because I remembered how in school they kept saying: "Stop daydreaming and concentrate!" And they said that your fingertips had to memorize the letters so that it would feel as if they were part of the machine. And at first it seemed so strange, because everything was pulling me away, away from the machine. And I really wanted to think about what was going on outside. There seemed so many things, though I can't recall them now. But they kept pushing me and pushing me: "Stop daydreaming! Concentrate!" And finally I did. And after a while it didn't seem so hard to do. And I won first prize in class. And the teacher said I'd have a real good choice in the jobs I could get because quality is always appreciated in this world and with quality you can get by.

And when I remembered how I'd sat doing those exercises making my fingertips memorize the letters, I was real mad because she was no different than the others. There's always something more. More for them. But not one notion about something more for me. Except maybe a better machine so that I can do more work more quickly. Or maybe a couple of hours less a week. That's the most that they can ever think of for me.

And I was so furious. I'd heard all this before. And I know that as soon as they tell you they'll fight to get you better working conditions, they go home and announce: "You couldn't pay me enough to do that kind of work." That's what they say behind your back.

And I started to yell at her: "If you got words and know what to say, how come you can't come up with something more for me?"

And she was so startled. I could see it in her eyes. I mean you've got to have nerve. I'm supposed to just stay here while she writes about me and my work.

And then I said: "They're always going to need people to type the final copies. And I can see you'll never waste your time with that once you've thought of all the right words." And she kind of backed up, because I must have looked really mad. And she bumped into the file cabinet and couldn't move back any further. And I said to her: "What's the difference to me? It's all the same. I always end up doing the same thing. So let's make it clear between us. Whenever you finish whatever it is you're writing about me and my work, don't count on me to help you out in the final stages. Never count on me, no matter how good the working conditions."

A Poem for Judy
beginning a new job

I will keep this simple
not give it
universal significance
nor transform it
into art.

You say:
"I will not do this
forever. I *will* paint."

I've learned now
that it's no solace
to point out   the others
so many others
straining   wasting
unable to do
what they know
they must do

for such loss
is always solitary
and unshared
outside the scope
of bloodless theory.

You do not paint
and what must happen
does not happen:
the transformation

on the empty canvas
of the elusive marble
into the shadowy water
or of the simple water
into impenetrable rock

and nothing
nothing
not even a loving embrace
nor special intimate
midnight talk
will ever make up
or diminish
that loss
for you
or for her
or her
or her

or her.

III

URBAN FLOWERS

Mnemonic Devices:
Brooklyn Botanic Gardens, 1981

1.

I'd forgotten. Despite the planters
blossoming in the northern light
despite the potted succulents
over which you take such care
and patience   despite the window boxes
wired to the crumbling ledges
I'd forgotten.

This morning   at the pond's edge   we watch
the energetic ducks   chase and fly
in enigmatic patterns. I declare it
a mating dance — an educated guess —
having lost the thread of cycles
seasons   time   except when April's
sharp insistent air   distracts us
from this city's bitter dream
and we rise one morning   and remember:

there are still the gardens.

2.

It is a ritual   for us
this annual return
to the unsuppressed spring
in this guarded landscape
to the flowers   and trees
earth   rocks   pond.

It is the stuff of mythology
both old and new   as we relive
once more   a certain day
suddenly grown   strange
and dim   and how we stood
uncertain and afraid
of the exploding lightning
and the silent trees.

That day   awakened in us images
long lost   amid the dangers
of the city streets   and
we stood amazed   at the sight
and sound   wondering
what else   we'd lost.

That day   the gardens
drenched in violent rains
were transformed   into a raw
uncultivated place. And we
were   wearied wanderers
dazed   in awe   having suddenly
stumbled into our native land.

Royal Pearl

Where do new varieties come from?
General Eisenhower is a red tulip which was first
recognized in 1951.
In 1957 a lemon yellow mutation appeared in a field of
red General Eisenhower tulips. This yellow mutation proved
to be a stable sport which was called — Royal Pearl.

BROOKLYN BOTANIC GARDENS

In dead of winter   imprisoned within
the imprisoned earth   it was a leap
defiant   of all eternal laws   and patterns.
Beneath the frozen earth   it came to be
like a splitting of an inner will
a wrenching from a designated path
a sudden burst   from a cause unknown.
And then in spring   it opened: a lemon yellow
in a pure red field.

Our words deny the simple beauty
the wild energy of the event. *Anomaly*
deviant   mutant   we're always taught
as though this world   were a finished place
and we the dull guardians   of its perfected forms.
Our lives are rooted in such words.

Yet each winter   there are some
who watch   the gardens   emptied
only white   as the snow presses
on the fenced-in grounds   just
as on an unclaimed field.
And each winter   there are some
who dream   of a splitting of an inner will
a wrenching from the designated path
who dream a purple flower   standing solitary
in a yellow field.

Lithops

Common name: living stone

Barely differentiated
from the inorganic   they conceal
their passions   in sheer survival.
It is philosophy: life's hard
growth and erosion   even rocks
in the end   are broken down
to formless dust.

But like all schema   incomplete
for between the grey and fleshy
crevices   strange blossoms grow
in brazen colors. For us it is
the ancient sign   that every life
has its secret longings   to transcend
the daily pressing need
longings   that one day   must flower.

Aesthetics

No beauty for beauty's sake here.
Life's too lean
a constant   "Let's get down
to brass tacks." Function and necessity.
Stone and water.

Like the popularity of narcissus bulbs
this season. Not as you'd expect
for the plant itself   which sprouts
endless green stalks   that rise up
stiff and straight   and then finally
eke out a few buds of puny white flowers.
Nor for the obvious lesson by example:
the unavoidable six weeks (maybe more)
of patient preparation   before
any real prospects of blooming.

But rather   for the roots beneath.
Brown tipped and firm   they probe
and press around the artificial stones
in intricate networks   even dead-end mazes
daring anyone to trace them back
to their original source. In the stores
the saleswomen warn: "They can toss
the stones right out of the container!"
And here   that remains the real attraction.

Winter Light

Almost December.   Indifferent
to seasons   the marigolds
persist. I am surprised by their pluck
and lack of propriety
their ability to ignore
the inappropriate:
a rusted leaking window box
a shaky fire escape
leading to a cemented street
below. They do not mourn
that all good things must
come to an end   and accept
that end as fate or destiny.
Instead   without struggle
or assessment of soil
moisture   heat   air   they continue
blooming   in chilling winter light
exactly as they did all summer.

Oleander

A gift from a lover when things
were definitely   going downhill.
"It's poisonous," she said.
"No known antidotes."
After the breakup   long after
when I'd already settled down
with someone else   I boarded it
with my mother   who's always taught:
never throw anything out.

Whenever I see it   I am drawn again
to the dissembling innocence   among the dark
green jade and purple passion. I long
to taste one leaf   one petal   to test
that warning   for nothing   I tell myself
not even death   could be that final.
You must understand   it is more
than mortal resistance
for there was a time   when she left
and I knew   was fiercely certain
this departure   was the last.

Cactus

for my mother
Rose Perczykow Klepfisz

The pot itself was half the story.
A yellow ceramic dime store knickknack
of a featureless Mexican
with a large sombrero   pushing a wagon
filled with dirt.

The cactus was the other half.
Self-effacing   it didn't demand much
which was just as well
since she had no spare time
for delicate cultivation.
Used to just the bare essentials
it stood on our kitchen windowsill
two floors above the inhospitable soil
and neither flourished   grew
nor died.

I'd catch her eyeing it
as she stood   breathless
broiling our dinner's minute steaks
her profile centered in the window frame.
She understood   the meaning   of both pot
and plant   still would insist there was
something extra   the colors yellow
green   or as she once explained
in her stiff night-school English:
"It is always of importance to see
the things aesthetical."

Abutilon in Bloom

for Diana Bellessi

Abutilon: flowering indoor maple;
houseplant

Cultivated inside   out of the bounds
of nature   it stubborned
on the windowsill   six winters and springs
resisting water   sun   all researched care.
It would not give   beyond its leaves.

Yet today   in the morning light
the sudden color asserts itself
among the spotted green   and I
pause   before another empty day
and wonder at its wild blooming.

It leans against the sunwarm glass
its blossoms firm on the thick stems
as if its roots
absorbed the knowledge
that there is no other place
that memory is only pain
that even here   now
we must burst forth with orange flowers
with savage hues of our captivity.

IV
....

INHOSPITABLE SOIL

> *i can't go back*
> *where i came from was*
> *burned off the map*
>
> *i'm a jew*
> *anywhere is someone else's land*
>   MELANIE KAYE/KANTROWITZ

Glimpses of the Outside

in memory of Marcia Tillotson (1940–1981)

A place

1.

Cherry Plain was once called South Berlin   before
the war   and then they probably became self-conscious.
Many here   go back before the Revolution   are of
Hessian descent   fought with the British. They are
wary of strangers   defined as anyone who has not lived
here since birth. Still they chat politely   wave
as I drive by. The children are more open   stare
shamelessly   at the new woman in town. It is a quiet
place. One post office. One small general store.
It could have grown and developed   when they expanded
old Route 22. But it would have meant   cutting into
the cemetery   and of course   that was out of the question.
Like disgruntled children   they protest over their parents'
limitations   for they see   they could have gotten something
off the weekenders   rushing back and forth on Friday
and Sunday nights. But ancestors will have their way.
So 22 looped around it   leaving the town intact   except
for the occasional stranger   who is looking for a way out.

2.

I have decided not to plant a garden   only to scavenge.
Already last year's furrows   (the result of others'
labor)   are vague   and the borders almost completely
obscured by the undisciplined   self-absorbed growth.
It is what we know of weeds: no delicate sense of
intrusion   of transgressing bounds. They move in
take over   and that's that. It doesn't bother me
this unreflecting rudeness. I am satisfied to witness
the few carrot sprigs   onions   tiny lettuce heads
and without commitment   to clear weedless islands
around them. The asparagus reaches its full growth
merges with the stalk   and goes to seed. The delicate
dill   follows suit   achieves its natural toughness.
I do not intercede   in these events.

3.

This house was once a meeting hall   then a dance
hall   a polling place. More recently   a garage.
I want to plant flowers around its edges   bring
to life an image   I have had about it. But the
earth is naturally tough with rocks   and more   it
is clogged with rusted screws and washers   spark plugs
colored chips of glass   all conspiring against my
trowel. Then too there is the heavy oil   already
congealed   fixed and unyielding   like ancient geological
strata. The inner image long forgotten   I tense
against this human resistance   push harder towards
an earlier time   towards less polluted soil.

4.

I have started transplanting wildflowers   whose
names I do not know. Small blue ones from a lake
in a state park. They are modest   with pale yellow
centers   used to the moisture of the water's edge.
I douse them every morning to make them feel at home.
From a roadside   I dig out bright yellow ones   plant
them by the unpainted barn   so I can see them from my
window as I work. These thrive   as if their sole pur-
pose   was my pleasure. But exotic   tall purple flowers
with bulb-type roots   strong like twine in their tie
to the earth   and to their particular spot   these shrivel
up a few hours after being placed by the barn. I consider
the possibilities: individual will   personality   simple
biochemical makeup. Whatever. These do not adapt.
They stand tall   and elegant   dried by the sun   next to
the brilliant yellow flowers   for whom a place by the barn
is as good   as a road bank.

5.

Midnight: the meadow is sparkling with fireflies.
I had always thought   that at night   they folded their
wings   over their iridescent bodies   and darkened
that light. Yet here they are   in constant motion
lighting against the shadow of the mountain. The
memory suddenly comes alive   like the underside of
a non-living stone. I am eight years old   and it is
almost dusk. The fireflies rush   through arid city
air. I trap them in a milk bottle   hoping to create
a lantern to light my way home. I do not understand
that not even the dusty grass hurriedly pressed through
the narrow bottleneck   will keep them alive   that
inevitably   in such confinement (is it a lack of air
or simply a lack of space for flight?)   their light will
dim and die.

6.

What could go wrong in such a setting? I ask
myself   thinking of that arid air   left behind
of the wino sleeping in my doorway   every night.
This valley   is so quiet   so clear and sharp-
edged   in the summer daylight. The old houses
meticulously painted   and the lawns carefully mowed
declare only: order and plain living. What could
go wrong in such a setting? I ask myself again.
The mountains look permanent   eternal in fact
though all I read about human life   about natural
evolution   tells me everything is in constant
motion   that this landscape was once of a different
sort   that these people who distrust strangers
were once strangers themselves   that the sign
"Indian Massacre Road"   a sign indistinguishable
from any other in lettering and color   posted modestly
at an obscure crossing   is but a barely noticeable
vestige   of one history forgotten and unattended.

7.

The pump is old   its age reflected in its weight
iron   shaped and welded more than a half a century ago.
It draws the water noisily   slowly   sounding like
a failing heart   pounding against itself. The plumbers
cluck their tongues   in masculine admiration. "She's
a goddamn antique" the young one says. He is tall
and handsome   with clear blue eyes. "Don't make those
anymore" he continues   with a voice of experience
his age denies. I suspect he's only an apprentice   for
he descends into the well   while the older man sits
casually on the ledge   occasionally offering advice.
They're in agreement   or in cahoots. Get a new pump.
This one's definitely shot. Not worth fixing   the parts
too difficult to find   and when found   too expensive.
I decide against it   at least for now   and tell them
to see if anything can be done. Later   I return and
ask   if they can patch it up. "Sure"   the young one
answers. "I'll take anything on   as long as it's white."

A visit

1.

The woman who is coming to visit   is my mother.
Her life   has been bracketed by historical events
over which she's had no control. During World War II
she developed a canniness for detecting Jews   did
not care how many documents they had to prove   who
they were not. She knew. She could tell   by a special
look in their eyes   a gesture of the hand   a confidence
too casual. This acquired ability   so finely tuned
during the war years   remains alive   so that today
decades later   she cannot wander far from her Jewish
neighborhood   before she begins assessing   who are
the safe ones   and who are not.

2.

Her survival   (and as a result mine)   was partly
dependent on: her small nose   her grey eyes. And
most critical: her impeccable Polish   (with no trace
of a Yiddish accent) because an older sister had
insisted she attend Polish schools   to gain greater
mobility. It was one perspective on the Jewish condition
in Poland. At critical moments   these elements   heredity
and environment   combined in the right proportions to
create luck. But there was also another: character
or in this case   guts. When the Germans came for her
she begged: *Ich habe ein kleines kind*. And when she
saw   the sliver of hesitation in their eyes   she ran
and took her chances. They did not chase   or shoot
just let her go. For months   she convinced the peasants
she was a Pole   playing a part   ad-libbing the dialogue
without a flaw   pretending to be the human being   they
assumed she was. During this time   she learned survival
depends on complete distrust. Even today   she is still
fierce   in her refusal to rely on others. Some would call
it alienation. Others pride. I think   it's only
the necessary stance   of any survivor.

3.

History   she says with irony   has a way of repeating
itself. *Then*   she outwitted two German soldiers   probably
young men   taught from childhood   the hideousness of
Jews. Faced with a woman   fair and ordinary   pleading
for her sickly child who would be orphaned   they must have
thought: No   this cannot be that Jewish monster. And
she escaped. At least momentarily. *Now*   she is trapped
again. But no walls or barbed wire   around her this time.
No plans for uprisings   or secret meetings. Each evening
she returns   hurrying through the orderly streets   ominous
in their emptiness   and steps into the elevator. I want
to offer her advice   strategy   a philosophy   but know their
utter uselessness in this age. For *now*   is a vastly
different time and place. The country is not occupied
by strangers. Those she fears most   are not an enemy.
And neglect and hunger   cannot be outwitted.

4.

We visit the Hancock Shaker Village   walking through
the restored buildings   recreated workrooms and living
quarters. I note the quietness   the simplicity of
the line   and wonder about the eye that fashioned it
the aesthetic vision   the philosophy of light   air
of raising the struggle for survival   above humiliation.
We pass through the herb garden. My mother stops
looks in amazement at the round stone barn   and marvels
how all this could have come to a dead stop   without
catastrophe   without disaster. She scrutinizes the
photographs of children   adopted and nurtured. "How
could they not have wanted children of their own?"
she asks   having always believed   that one's own blood is
the sole source   of all security. And I see her shift
as she tells me again   of the children   hidden in convents
baptized and converted   then claimed by relatives after
the war. Many were finally kidnapped   by their protectors
bribed and bought off. Some could never be reclaimed.
For those who were   it was hard   painful   but my mother
adds   "They were our only hope."

5.

But it is not simply a question of reproduction
I tell myself that night   thinking of my own child-
lessness. They lacked something   which would have
pushed them on   which would have given them   a hook
in time. But it was time itself   that they ignored
thinking the farmland and woods   around the village
the seasons emerging predictably   in full character
the day and the night   all these   they assumed were
heaven   eternal. At the end of each day   after baking
and laundry   welding and weaving   tending the children
and the fields   they would meet   and reaffirm their faith.
First they shook out the sins from their bodies   then
danced holding their palms up   to gather in the blessings.
There was no time   there was no death. And so they
lived   and so they died.

6.

My mother boards the train   and sits behind the
tinted glass. She mouths words and gestures   nothing
I can understand. I raise my arms in frustration
motion her to try again. She does   but the barriers
remain. She writes a note   on a piece of paper   holds
it against the glass. The European script is clear:
"It is empty here. It is cool." I smile   and give
the okay sign. She will be comfortable on her trip back
to the city. Still   I am all anxiety. Departures
swell old   undefined fears in me   the fear of permanent
separations. Old   long-forgotten departures   which
remain active in me   like instinct. The fear of being
lost and never found   of losing all trace   all connections
severed   the thread broken. (When after two years   she
came to get me from the orphanage   I cried when I caught
sight of her   and raised my arms to her. I was barely
three   but I had not forgotten.) Of endless   futile
searches for relatives long vanished   or even worse
alive   but not traceable.

The train begins to move. My mother sits behind the
tinted glass and waves. Her face becomes an angle   and
then disappears. Her words were: "Find a place where
you are happy." But the sound of those words   had
the mourning of separation.

A place in time

1.

The postmistress is insecure in her calculations.
She checks   and rechecks all her figures never having
the ease of certainty. Still   I trust her view
of this place   for she has that tutored eye   able to
detect the changes   nuances and variations   whose
implications   remain obscure to my alien reasoning.
She is chatty   inquisitive. Sometimes   I think she must
be lonely   sitting all day by herself   behind the old-
fashioned post office boxes   decorated with elaborate
brass eagles. Perhaps the grocery will be sold (and then
we'll be stuck   with whoever buys it). Perhaps the mail
truck will be traded in   (and then we'll have regular
delivery). Perhaps the church will be painted   by early
fall (and we can begin having services again). Perhaps
the rumors about the metal barrels   buried in the nearby
campgrounds are true   (and we should stop swimming
in that lake).

2.

At first   the cats were cautious   flattening
themselves   along the ground   slinking close to
the edges of the house. No vestigial recollections
springing from the unconscious depth of the species.
Or so I thought. But now   and I can hardly measure
the time elapsed   they act as if it's all they've
ever known   routinely bringing in mice from the meadow
or bodies of birds   necks snapped   heads hanging
like colored limp sacks. I glimpse my favorite
the tortoise shell   eating a rabbit   whose belly seems
expertly slashed and exposed. She hunches   over it
calmly chewing   the juicy red meat   patiently breaking
through   the sinewy flesh.

3.

At the Burr & Grille in Averill Park   only men
are at the bar. They look like mechanics: oil-
streaked pants   work gloves stuffed in pockets.
They swap army stories   their glimpses of the
outside. In Haiti   I overhear   there are only
the rich and the poor. "Nothing in the middle"
a man in his twenties says. The rich live on top
of the mountain   the poor by the sea. They earn
about $35 a year. "Imagine the kind of life   *that*
is. They're starving. Imagine! In this day and age!"
Burr   behind the bar   clucks his tongue. "In China"
he says   "they fight over candy bars. Imagine what
that must be like." The young one begins again
"You know   you get off   and they have all those
bands and colorful costumes   and everything is all
welcome. And then you take five steps away from
the pier   and *wham!* [he bangs his hand down on the bar]
they're ready to slit your throat   to get that wallet!"

4.

Saturday: The Baptist Church flea market and auction
offers the predictable merchandise. Old clothes
battered pots and pans   chipped glassware   rusted lawn
furniture. "It's all for a good cause"   a woman tells
me   and mentions interior renovations. I wonder if I'm
the only Jew in the crowd. An older man approaches.
"Smile!" he orders. "The Lord loves you! Certainly
the Lord loves you!" I nod   feel uncomfortable   move
towards another table. A woman   about seven months
pregnant   is having her purchases priced. She is no
more than twenty   with a small pale face   faintly freckled
deeply worn. Dressed in colorless bermudas   and a gray
blouse   she holds a carton of baby clothes. On the ground
by her feet are cheap games of plastic   a round container
with broken wooden logs   the debris of an old erector set.
This too   is her collection   the necessary response
to life's gnawing insistence on itself   on not being
ignored. She looks wearied   almost emptied by her vigilance.
I watch as she hands over the $10 bill and waits
for the change   watch   as she smiles and turns away.

5.

I ride the backroads   far from any village or town
far from the blacktops   carefully numbered. Woods
along both sides. Suddenly   I am startled by an
unexpected home   a trailer on a small patch of cleared
land. Logic would say   that it had no stability
the cinderblocks at its corners appearing flimsy   unable
to keep it firmly rooted to the ground. Yet the faded
paint   the obvious rust creeping along its outer shell
reveal a hard-won permanence. Barefoot children stop
playing in front of a torn screen door   stand anxious
tentative   waiting for the unfamiliar car to pass.
A woman's eyes   keep guard at a kitchen window. Plastic
deer and clay ducks line the worn path. Junked cars
spill out of the collapsed garage. Gray overalls   and
bright sheets with sunsets   dry between two shade trees.
In a carved-out tractor tire   painted red and white   grow
yellow marigolds   blue petunias. An orderly vegetable
garden on one side   loose piles of freshly split logs
on the other   testify to the implacable needs of winter.
All is urgency   asymmetry in this territory resistant
to maps and philosophy. Only the seasons   and birth
and death   remain stark. I know   I see   I learn again
from the anxiety in that woman's eyes   in the caution
of the children's stance   that there is no escape.

Mourning

1.

I reread his letter. He writes about your struggle
Marcia   your will to survive. I read the letter again
and stare at the mountain's outline   behind the house.
It is will   against the dark shadowy mountain   that I
keep thinking about. How you refused   up to the last
moment   refused to say   it is over   but stretched out
your time   how you were willing to endure the pain   how
you would not be separated from it   because it alone
held the possibility of life. A few days before you died
a friend said: *Everything's collapsing   but she simply
refuses.* I think about that refusal to cooperate   to give
yourself an easeful death. It is your will   Marcia
I am trying to understand.

2.

Why so hard to absorb   after all the waiting?
The daily calls   and reports   turned your body
into a machine. The nurses were polite   precise.
Respiratory arrest. Cardiac failure. She's
breathing on her own now. Somewhat better.
"How is her spirit?" I ask stupidly   as if
the answer could make a bond between us. One
time they said: She is angry.   Another: She is
somewhat anxious.

3.

Death asserts itself as everywhere   pulls me out
of the eternal   roots me in this time   in this place.
Your death   Marcia. After thirteen years of struggles
who would have thought   this was the final one   who
would have thought   this one was different   from all
the others? It is something I must plant   I keep saying
as if I could contain the loss   by finding the right
piece of ground   by the barn perhaps   or by the gigantic
ash   that hovers over the house   a tree planted by
a neighbor's father   more than sixty years ago. I
need a place for your death   Marcia   for it feels like
an emptiness   that can erode   all the mountains
that protect this valley.

4.

But there is no possibility of containing it. All
the days merge   and only hindsight   reveals the subtle
but discrete changes: the shortened daylight
the slowly   yellowing grass. I place seeds in the bird
feeder   write letters home   check the final stages of
the garden's undisciplined growth. Everything is
shriveling   emptying itself of body and substance
huddling closer and closer to the earth. I plant bulbs
like a skeptic   never fully believing   these drab
lifeless lumps   will bloom next year   in full exotic color.
Nothing   I think   staring at the sixty-year-old ash
should be taken for granted. I push my trowel   deeper
sift out the slivers of glass   the heavy nails   place
the bulbs in their designated places   then cover them
with soil   flattening the surface with my hand.

Bashert

These words are dedicated to those who died

These words are dedicated to those who died
because they had no love and felt alone in the world
because they were afraid to be alone and tried to stick it out
because they could not ask
because they were shunned
because they were sick and their bodies could not resist the
disease
because they played it safe
because they had no connections
because they had no faith
because they felt they did not belong and wanted to die

These words are dedicated to those who died
because they were loners and liked it
because they acquired friends and drew others to them
because they took risks
because they were stubborn and refused to give up
because they asked for too much

These words are dedicated to those who died
because a card was lost and a number was skipped
because a bed was denied
because a place was filled and no other place was left

bashert (Yiddish): inevitable, (pre)destined

These words are dedicated to those who died
because someone did not follow through
because someone was overworked and forgot
because someone left everything to God
because someone was late
because someone did not arrive at all
because someone told them to wait and they just couldn't
any longer

These words are dedicated to those who died
because death is a punishment
because death is a reward
because death is the final rest
because death is eternal rage

These words are dedicated to those who died

Bashert

These words are dedicated to those who survived

These words are dedicated to those who survived
because their second grade teacher gave them books
because they did not draw attention to themselves and got lost
in the shuffle
because they knew someone who knew someone else who could
help them and bumped into them on a corner on a Thursday
afternoon
because they played it safe
because they were lucky

These words are dedicated to those who survived
because they knew how to cut corners
because they drew attention to themselves and always got
picked
because they took risks
because they had no principles and were hard

These words are dedicated to those who survived
because they refused to give up and defied statistics
because they had faith and trusted in God
because they expected the worst and were always prepared
because they were angry
because they could ask
because they mooched off others and saved their strength
because they endured humiliation
because they turned the other cheek
because they looked the other way

These words are dedicated to those who survived
because life is a wilderness and they were savage
because life is an awakening and they were alert
because life is a flowering and they blossomed
because life is a struggle and they struggled
because life is a gift and they were free to accept it

These words are dedicated to those who survived

Bashert

1. Poland, 1944: My mother is walking down a road

My mother is walking down a road. Somewhere in Poland. Walking towards an unnamed town for some kind of permit. She is carrying her Aryan identity papers. She has left me with an old peasant who is willing to say she is my grandmother.

She is walking down a road. Her terror in leaving me behind, in risking the separation is swallowed now, like all other feelings. But as she walks, she pictures me waving from the dusty yard, imagines herself suddenly picked up, the identity papers challenged. And even if she were to survive that, would she ever find me later? She tastes the terror in her mouth again. She swallows.

I am over three years old, corn-silk blond and blue-eyed like any Polish child. There is terrible suffering among the peasants. Starvation. And like so many others, I am ill. Perhaps dying. I have bad lungs. Fever. An ugly ear infection that oozes pus. None of these symptoms are disappearing.

The night before, my mother feeds me watery soup and then sits and listens while I say my prayers to the Holy Mother, Mother of God. I ask her, just as the nuns taught me, to help us all: me, my mother, the old woman. And then catching myself, learning to use memory, I ask the Mother of God to help my father. The Polish words slip easily from my lips. My mother is satisfied. The peasant has perhaps heard and is reassured. My mother has found her to be kind, but knows that she is suspicious of strangers.

My mother is sick. Goiter. Malnutrition. Vitamin deficiencies. She has skin sores which she cannot cure. For months now she has been living in complete isolation, with no point of reference outside of herself. She has been her own sole advisor, companion, comforter. Almost everyone of her world is dead: three sisters, nephews, and nieces, her mother, her husband, her in-laws. All gone. Even the remnants of the resistance, those few left after the uprising, have dispersed into the Polish countryside. She is more alone than she could have ever imagined. Only she knows her real name and she is perhaps dying. She is thirty years old.

I am over three years old. I have no consciousness of our danger, our separateness from the others. I have no awareness that we are playing a part. I only know that I have a special name, that I have been named for the Goddess of Peace. And each night, I sleep secure in that knowledge. And when I wet my bed, my mother places me on her belly and lies on the stain. She fears the old woman and hopes her body's warmth will dry the sheet before dawn.

My mother is walking down a road. Another woman joins her. My mother sees through the deception, but she has promised herself that never, under any circumstances, will she take that risk. So she swallows her hunger for contact and trust and instead talks about the sick child left behind and lies about the husband in the labor camp.

Someone is walking towards them. A large, strange woman with wild red hair. They try not to look at her too closely, to seem overly curious. But as they pass her, my mother feels something move inside her. The movement grows and grows till it is an explosion of yearning that she cannot contain. She stops, orders her companion to continue without her. And then she turns.

The woman with the red hair has also stopped and turned. She is grotesque, bloated with hunger, almost savage in her rags. She and my mother move towards each other. Cautiously, deliberately, they probe past the hunger, the swollen flesh, the infected skin, the rags. Slowly, they begin to pierce five years of encrusted history. And slowly, there is perception and recognition.

In this wilderness of occupied Poland, in this vast emptiness where no one can be trusted, my mother has suddenly, bizarrely, met one of my father's teachers. A family friend. Another Jew.

They do not cry, but weep as they chronicle the dead and count the living. Then they rush to me. To the woman I am a familiar sight. She calculates that I will not live out the week, but comments only on my striking resemblance to my father. She says she has contacts. She leaves. One night a package of food is delivered anonymously. We eat. We begin to bridge the gap towards life. We survive.

2. Chicago, 1964: I am walking home alone at midnight

I am walking home alone at midnight. I am a student of literature, and each night I stay in the library until it closes. Yet each night as I return, I still feel unprepared for the next day. The nature of literary movements eludes me. I only understand individual writers. I have trouble remembering genre definitions, historical dates and names, cannot grasp their meaning, significance. A whole world of abstractions and theories remains beyond my reach, on the other side of a wall I cannot climb over.

So each night, I walk home clutching my books as if I were a small school child. The city is alien. Since coming to America, this is my first time away from a Jewish neighborhood, Jewish friends, and I feel isolated, baffled at how to make a place for myself in this larger, gentile world which I have entered.

I am walking home alone at midnight. The university seems an island ungrounded. Most of its surrounding streets have been emptied. On some, all evidence of previous life removed except for occasional fringes of rubble that reveal vague outlines that hint at things that were. On others, old buildings still stand, though these are hollow like caves, once of use and then abandoned. Everything is poised. Everything is waiting for the emptiness to close in on itself, for the emptiness to be filled up, for the emptiness to be swallowed and forgotten.

Walking home, I am only dimly aware of the meaning of this strange void through which I pass. I am even less aware of the dangers for someone like me, a woman walking home alone at midnight. I am totally preoccupied with another time, another place. Night after night, protected by the darkness, I think only of Elza who is dead. I am trying to place a fact about her, a fact which stubbornly resists classification: nothing that happened to her afterwards mattered. All the agonized effort. All that caring. *None of that mattered!*

At the end of the war, friends come to claim her. With the cold, calculated cunning of an adult, the eight year old vehemently denies who she is. No she is not who they think. Not a Jew. They have made a mistake. Mixed her up with another Elza. This one belongs here, with her mother.

She is simply being scrupulous in following her parents' instructions. "Do not ever admit to anyone who you are. It is our secret. Eventually we will come for you. Remember! *Never admit who you are!* Promise!"

Four years later, the war is over. Her parents are dead. She is still bound by her promise. This woman is her mother. Her parents' friends know better. The woman has been kind, has saved her. But she is a Pole and Elza is a Jew. Finally, the bribe is big enough and the child released. Elza becomes an orphan.

And afterwards? She is adopted and finally seems to have everything. Two parents. Two handsome brothers. A house. Her own room. She studies Latin and does translations. Is valedictorian of her class. Goes away to college. Has boyfriends, affairs. Comes to New York. Works. Begins graduate school. Explicates Dylan Thomas, T. S. Eliot. Marries.

But none of it matters. She cannot keep up. The signs are clear. She is a poor housekeeper. Insists they eat off paper plates. She buys enough clothes to fill all her closets. But nothing soothes her. Finally she signs her own papers. Is released within a few months. I finish college and leave for Europe. Three weeks later, she checks into a hotel and takes an overdose. She is twenty-five years old.

Fearing I too might be in danger, my mother instructs Polish Jews resettled in Paris and Tel Aviv: "Don't tell her!" And to me she writes: "Elza is in the hospital again. There is no hope." I am suspicious, refer to her whenever I can. I am alert. Sense a discomfort, an edge I cannot define. I think I know, but I never dare ask. I come home. Seven months after her death, I finally know.

A story she once told me remains alive. During the war, the Polish woman sends her to buy a notebook for school. She is given the wrong change and points it out. The shopkeeper eyes her sharply: "Very accurate. Just like a Jew. Perhaps you are a little Jewess?" And Elza feels afraid and wonders if this woman sees the truth in her blue eyes.

Another memory: Elza is reading accounts of the war. She cannot help herself she tells me. An anecdote explains something to her. A woman in a camp requests a bandage for a wound. And the guard, so startled by her simplicity and directness, makes sure she gets one. That woman, Elza tells me, refused to stop acting like a human being. Jews, she concludes, made a terrible mistake.

I am walking home alone at midnight. I am raw with the pain of her death. I wonder. Is it inevitable? Everything that happened to us afterwards, to all of us, does none of it matter? Does it not matter what we do and where we live? Are there moments in history which cannot be escaped or transcended, but which act like time warps permanently trapping all those who are touched by them? And that which should have happened in 1944 in Poland and didn't, must it happen now? In 1964? In Chicago? Or can history be tricked and cheated?

These questions haunt me. Yet I persist with a will I myself do not understand. I continue reading, studying, making friends. And as the rawness of Elza's death eases and becomes familiar, as time becomes distance, I find myself more and more grounded in my present life, in my passion for words and literature. I begin to perceive the world around me. I develop perspective.

I see the rubble of this unbombed landscape, see that the city, like the rest of this alien country, is not simply a geographic place, but a time zone, an era in which I, by my very presence in it, am rooted. No one simply passes through. History keeps unfolding and demanding a response. A life obliterated around me of those I barely noticed. A life unmarked, unrecorded. A silent mass migration. Relocation. Common rubble in the streets.

I see now the present dangers, the dangers of the void, of the American hollowness in which I walk calmly day and night as I continue my life. I begin to see the incessant grinding down of lines for stamps, for jobs, for a bed to sleep in, of a death stretched imperceptibly over a lifetime. I begin to understand the ingenuity of it. The invisibility. The Holocaust without smoke.

Everything is poised. Everything is waiting for the emptiness to be filled up, for the filling-up that can never replace, that can only take over. Like time itself. Or history.

3. Brooklyn, 1971: I am almost equidistant from two continents

I am almost equidistant from two continents. I look back towards one, then forward towards the other. The moment is approaching when I will be equidistant from both and will have to choose. Maintaining equidistance is not a choice.

By one of those minor and peculiar coincidences that permanently shape and give texture to our lives, I am born on my father's twenty-eighth birthday. Two years later, exactly three days after his thirtieth and my second birthday, he is dead in the brush factory district of the Warsaw Ghetto. His corpse is buried in a courtyard and eventually the spot blends with the rest of the rubble. The Uprising, my birth, his death — all merge and become interchangeable. That is the heritage of one continent.

In one of the classes that I teach, all the students are Black and Puerto Rican. I am the only white. Initially, the students are nervous, wondering if I will be a hard taskmaster. I am nervous too, though I do not yet have a name for it. After a few months together, we grow accustomed to each other. I am trying to understand my role here. That is the heritage of the other continent.

And now, approaching my own thirtieth birthday, approaching the moment when I will be equidistant from the two land masses, I feel some kind of cellular breakdown in my body, a sudden surging inside me, as if flesh and muscle and bone were losing definition. Everything in me yearns to become transparent, to be everywhere, to become like the water between two vast land masses that will never touch. I desire to become salt water, to establish the connection.

I am almost equidistant from two continents.

April 17, 1955. I have been asked to light one of the six candles. I stand on the stage in the large, darkened auditorium, wait to be called, wait to accept the flame, to pass it on like a memory. I am numb with terror at the spectacle around me. I fear these people with blue numbers on their arms, people who are disfigured and scarred, who have missing limbs and uneasy walks, people whose histories repel me. Here in this auditorium, they abandon all inhibitions, they transform themselves into pure sound, the sound of irretrievable loss, of wild pain and sorrow. Then they become all flesh, wringing their hands and covering their swollen eyes and flushed faces. They call out to me and I feel myself dissolving.

When it is time for me to come forward, to light the candle for those children who were burned, who were shot, who were stomped to death, I move without feeling. And as I near the candelabra, I hear them call out the common Yiddish names: *Surele. Moyshele. Channele. Rivkele. Yankele. Shayndele. Rayzl. Benyomin. Chavele. Miriam. Chaim.* The names brush against my face, invade my ears, my mouth. I breathe them into my lungs, into my bones. And as the list continues, guided by their sounds, I cross the stage and light the sixth and final candle. It is my fourteenth birthday.

I am almost equidistant from two continents.

March, 1971. There are twenty-eight people in the class. Eighteen women, ten men. Some married. Some single. Alone. With children. With parents and grandparents. Nieces. Nephews. They are here because they have not met the minimum standards of this college. This class is their special chance to catch up. Subject and verb agreement. Sentence fragments. Pronoun reference. Vocabulary building. Paragraph organization. Topic sentence. Reading comprehension. Study skills. Discipline. All this to catch up, or as one student said to me, his eyes earnest: "I want to write so that when I go for a job they won't think I'm lazy."

I am required to take attendance. I check through the names, call them out each morning: *James. Reggie. Marie. Simone. Joy. Christine. Alvarez. Ashcroft. Basile. Colon. Corbett. White. Raphael. Dennis. Juan. Carissa. Lamont. Andrea.* Fragments of their lives fall before me. The chaos and disorganization. A mother needing help in filling out forms in English. A sick child. Hospital regulations. A brother looking for a job. Another brother in trouble. Welfare red tape. Unemployment payment restrictions. Waiting lists. Eviction. SRO. The daily grind interrupting their catching-up, and the increasing sense that with each day missed, they fall further behind.

I am almost equidistant from two continents. I look back towards one, then forward towards the other. There is a need in me to become transparent like water, to become the salt water which is their only connection.

March, 1971. Marie wants to study medicine. She concedes it's a long haul, but, as she says, "It's only time. What difference does it make?" Slightly older than the others, she lives alone with her daughter. To some of the women's horror, she refuses to have a telephone, does not like to be intruded upon. When necessary, she can always be reached through a neighbor. She rarely misses class, on a few occasions brings her daughter with her who sits serenely drawing pictures. Facing Marie, I sometimes do not know who I am and wonder how she perceives me. She seems oblivious to my discomfort. She is only focused on the class, always reworking her assignments, reading everything twice, asking endless questions to make sure she really understands. One day, at the end of the hour, when we are alone, she asks: "What are you?" I am caught off guard, know the meaning of the question, but feel the resistance in me. I break it down and answer quietly: "A Jew." She nods and in that moment two vast land masses touch.

Each continent has its legacy. The day I reach my thirtieth birthday, the age of my father's death, I am equidistant from both. And as the moment passes, everything in me becomes defined again. I am once again muscle, flesh, bone. America is not my place of birth, not even my chosen home. Just a spot where it seemed safe to go to escape certain dangers. But safety, I discover, is only temporary. No place guarantees it to anyone forever. I have stayed because there is no other place to go. In my muscles, my flesh, my bone, I balance the heritages, the histories of two continents.

4. Cherry Plain, 1981: I have become a keeper of accounts

There are moments when I suddenly become breathless, as if I had just tricked someone, but was afraid the ruse would be exposed and I'd be hunted again. At those moments, the myths that propel our history, that turn fiction into fact, emerge in full force in me, as I stare into the eyes of strangers or someone suddenly grown alien. And when I see their eyes become pinpoints of judgments, become cold and indifferent, or simply distanced with curiosity, at those moments I hear again the words of the Polish woman:

Very accurate. Just like a Jew. You are perhaps a little Jewess?

At moments such as these I teeter, shed the present, and like rage, like pride, like acceptance, like the refusal to deny, I call upon the ancient myths again and say:

Yes. It's true. All true. I am scrupulously accurate. I keep track of all distinctions. Between past and present. Pain and pleasure. Living and surviving. Resistance and capitulation. Will and circumstances. Between life and death. Yes. I am scrupulously accurate. I have become a keeper of accounts.

Like the patriarchs, the shabby scholars who only lived for what was written and studied it all their lives

Like the inhuman usurers and dusty pawnbrokers who were quarantined within precisely prescribed limits of every European town and who were as accurate as the magistrates that drew the boundaries of their lives and declared them diseased

Like those men of stone who insisted that the *goyim* fulfill the contracts they had signed and who responded to the tearful pleas of illness, weakness, sudden calamity and poverty, with the words: "What are these to me? You have made me a keeper of accounts. Give me my pound of flesh. It says on this piece of paper, you owe me a pound of flesh!"

Like those old, heartless, dried-up merchants whose entire lives were spent in the grubby *shtetl* streets that are now but memory, whose only body softness was in their fingertips worn smooth by silver coins, whose vision that all that mattered was on pieces of paper was proven absolutely accurate, when their *złoty, francs,* and *marks* could not buy off the written words *Żyd, Juif, Jüde*

Like these, my despised ancestors
I have become a keeper of accounts.

And like all the matriarchs, the wives and daughters, the sisters and aunts,
the nieces, the keepers of button shops, milliners, seamstresses, peddlers of
foul fish, of matches, of rotten apples, laundresses, midwives, floor washers
and street cleaners, who rushed exhausted all week so that *shabes* could be
observed with fresh *khale* on the table, who argued in the common tongue

and begged for the daughter run off to the revolution
and the daughter run off with a *sheygets*
who refused to sit *shiva* and say *kadish* for a living child
who always begged for life
who understood the accounts but saw them differently
who knew the power of human laws, knew they always counted
no matter what the revolution or the party or the state
who knew the power of the words *Żyd, Juif, Jüde*

who cried whole lifetimes for their runaway children
for the husbands immobilized by the written word
for the brother grown callous from usury
for the uncle grown indifferent from crime, from bargaining,
from chiseling, from jewing them down

Like these, my despised ancestors
I have become a keeper of accounts.

I do not shun this legacy. I claim it as mine   whenever I see the
photographs of nameless people. Standing staring off the edge of
the picture. People dressed in coats lined with fur. Or ragged at
elbows and collar. Hats cocked on one side glancing anxiously
toward the lens. A peasant cap centered and ordinary. Hair styled
in the latest fashion. Or standing ashamed a coarse wig awk-
wardly fitted. The shabby clothes. Buttons missing. The elegant
stance. Diamond rings. Gold teeth. The hair being shaved. The
face of humiliation. The hand holding the child's hand. A tree. A
track. A vague building in a photograph. A facility. And then the
fields of hair   the endless fields of hair   the earth growing fertile
with their bodies   with their souls.

Old   rarely seen types. Gone   they say   forever. And yet I
know they can be revived again   that I can trigger them again.
That they awaken in me   for I have felt it happen   in the sight
of strangers   or someone suddenly grown alien. Whenever I have
seen the judgment   the coldness   and indifference   the
distanced curiosity.   At those moments   I teeter   shed my
present self   and all time merges   and like rage   like pride
like acceptance   like the refusal to deny   I answer

Yes. It is true.   I am keeper of accounts.

Bashert

Solitary Acts

for my aunt Gina Klepfisz (1908?–1942)

To garden is a solitary act.
MICHELLE CLIFF

1.

And to die
as you did   with the father
confessor   standing   waiting
patiently   for your death
for your final words
and you   watching the dissolution
around you   watching his eyes
his face   listening to his Latin words
said: "What have I to confess?
I am a Jew."

It was 1942   and you wanted someone
to know   though you'd be buried
in a Christian grave   with an Aryan name.

Such will to be known   can alter history.

2.

Today   I stand alone   planning my first garden
and think of you buried on that other continent
rescued from the Christian plot
the only flesh of your family   to lie
in a marked grave   in the Jewish cemetery
in a Warsaw   almost empty of any Jews.
That ground   I know   is but a fragment
of the past   a place apart   the surroundings
long rebuilt   into a modern city
and I know   that even now
while I stand   and try to map this season's growth
that country   cleansed of our people's blood
intones the litany of old complaints.

Gina   they hate us still.

3.

You are to me   everything
that remains   outside my grasp
everything   in this world
that is destroyed   with no one
there to rescue the fragments
to hear the words.
So much of history   seems
a gaping absence   at best a shadow
longing   for some greater
definition   which will never come
for what is burned   becomes air
and ashes   nothing more.

So I cling   to the knowledge of your
distant grave   for it alone
reminds me   prods me   to shape that shadow.

4.

I have spent a life   disentangling from influences
trying to claim   what was original   mine:
form my mother's mastery   of daily survival
so subtly interwoven   with common gestures
few recognize it   for what it is
from my father's more visibly   heroic deed
of dying   recorded in memoirs   tributes
from the deaths of grandparents   aunts   uncles
anonymous   in a heap   indistinguishable
from all the others   who died unmourned.

And now I remember you   and face another:
Gina   in those few months   when you watched
over me   before my consciousness learned
the danger   into which I had just been born
and the label   of who I was   and while my mother
sick and weak   teetered on the edge of life
in those few months   as the meaning of the ghetto
walls   grew more defined   as you inched people
out of the *umschlagplatz*   your chest contracting
gasping   with fear   yet certain that this needed to be done
I believe   that in that short time   something
passed between us   Gina   and you imparted to me
the vision   the firm sense of self   that gave
you strength   to state your name.

5.

And who would say   that I have mourned
enough   that I have looked at the old
photographs enough   yellowed and faded
and the green ink   now a grey dullness
where Marek   placed the flowers
on the rubble   where my father's body
was buried and disappeared   and Marek's head
looking down   his profile   etched against
an empty horizon   for there was nothing left

who would say   that I have mourned
enough?

And when I asked my mother if I
could have this album   that holds it all
holds more than most have   who are
without a witness   to mark their spot in green
or whose graves have been overgrown by weeds
or forests   or bulldozed for the sake
of modern cities   or whose bodies were never
buried   but were left for speechless animals
to devour   there is no piece of earth
that does not have its nameless   who lived
and died   unnoticed   beyond the grasp of history
who die today

And when I asked my mother   if I
could have this album   and she replied
this stays here   in this apartment
until I die   I glimpsed again the urgency
to be known.

6.

There have been many plots of ground
that formed me. This town's church
its cemetery   the bare   expectant earth
of my garden   all remind me   of that
other soil   on which I grew.

The first   was the green bush and grass
behind Marek's house in Łódź. It was
after the war   and Elza   orphaned   and just recently
claimed   from the Polish stranger   stood proud
before me   and brushed her long blond hair
her haughtiness   her only power. I watched
ashamed   and awkward   my small hand trying
to hide   my bald head   shaved for reasons
I was never told. It was our first meeting.

More than two years later   in the neutral
countryside that never saw the war   in Neglinge
Gaby and I   crawled flat on our stomachs
to see the miniature wildflowers   hidden
beneath the blooming lilac bush. They grew
for elves   I said   and bound him to me
with the secret   not wanting anyone else
to know. He was alert then   but only months
before   had refused to eat   was force fed
in a Stockholm hospital. When his appetite
returned   he clung to me   four years older
in a way   no one could ever understand
and I responded   as I never would again
unconsciously   selflessly   with complete
certainty.   I knew that he must live
and inched him along.

And again   a few years later   in a park   the Bronx
there was an unmowed field   near a metal fence.
My mother would bring me here   on warm summer Sundays
and spread a blanket   that would billow
over the high   resistant grass   then finally settle
and flatten with the weight of our bodies.
We brought things to read   books that warmed
with the sun   newspapers   that yellowed
as the day wore on.

These were the gardens of my childhood.

7.

Gina   I must tell you: today I
felt hopeful   as I knelt close
to the earth   and turned it
inch by inch   sifting the soil
clearing the way   for roots
of vegetables. I felt so hopeful
Gina   that with repeated years
and efforts   the monotony of daily
motion   of bending   and someday
the earth   would be uncluttered
the debris cleared.

There is   I know   no reason
for such hope   for nothing destroyed
is ever made up   or restored to us.
In the earth   are buried histories
irretrievable.   Yet what philosophy
can justify   any of our emotions?
Like the watercolors from Buchenwald —
if you can imagine! The stench
from the chimneys   just the sounds
of the place. And yet someone felt
a need to paint. And did.

So do not ask me to explain
why I draw meaning and strength
from these common gestures   why today
my hope is unwavering   solid   as if
I'd never lost it   or never would again
as if those dying   angry or stunned
at the stupidity of it   could be revived
as if their mortal wounds   could heal
as if their hunger   could be outlived
as if they were not dying   strangers
to others   strangers to themselves.

I need to hope. And do.

8.

I have been a dreamer   dreaming
of a perfect garden   of a family tree
whose branches   spread   through centuries
of an orderly cemetery   with no gravestones
missing. Tonight   as the sun sets   and I
turn towards evening   I have no such dreams.
Like the woman   who refused to trace
the ancient constellations   upon a clear
and crowded sky   because finding the stars
recording each in its place   the faint
and the brilliant   was enough
I too   Gina   have discarded all patterns
and blueprints. This night   I want only
to sleep   a dark   rich   dreamless sleep
to shelter   in me   what is left
to strengthen myself   for what is needed.

Cherry Plain, New York
August 1982

A Few Words in
the Mother Tongue

(1983–1990)

I cannot swim

I cannot swim   but my parents
say the land is less safe.   And
the first day   the water was smooth
like slate I could walk on.
It was a deception.

The sky greyed   darkened
then grew bright   as if it understood
our mood.   I watched the land sink
and disappear. The boat was firm.
I sat holding onto my father's leg.
I was not sick like the others.

The sky was bright   then grew
grey and dark. The days were
the same the water the same
and everyone's eyes the same.
We looked like a family   but
we were all strangers.   Nothing
but water and sky and the boat.
The world never existed I said.
I could not remember land   nor
houses nor trees and I knew
I had not been born here
that once there had been another place.
And I said to my parents
there are no more lands
and no more peoples.   We are strange
creatures and must grow gills.

And my parents laughed as I cupped
my hands around my ears and the
children laughed and did the same
their bony fingers flapping.
And the water looked gentle
ready to receive us.

And one day   we saw them   and I
saw we were not alone   and there
were others. Not sea creatures
but like us. I remembered.
And they boarded us and seized
the young girls like me and formed
a circle. And they were on us
when the leader shouted: Make
sounds of joy!   And my parents' eyes
sealed like wrinkled walnuts.
And they changed places   and new ones
were on us.   And someone ordered:
Make sounds of joy!   My parents moved
their lips like fishes   their mouths
filled with silence.   And it happened
again and again   to me   till I stopped
remembering it.

The blood clotted between the boards
and darkened.   Though the women splashed
the sea on it   the smell stayed.
I said to my parents: I will grow gills
and tried to leap out   into the water.
But my father held my wrists   his fingers
iron nails piercing my bones.   And he said:
you cannot swim.

The ocean was bleak and jagged
like an unscaled mountain   daring
to be conquered.   At dusk someone
spotted the land   but I did not look
at it   and watched my shadow below
on the rippled darkening bottom.

I thought about those who waited
on the shore. They were shouting
sharp   not kind   pointing at an empty
horizon.   Wood splintered wood   just
for one moment   and then they pushed
us back. My mother pressed my head
against her breast. The day was ending.
It was almost dark.

Di rayze aheym/The journey home

1. *Der fentster*/The window

She looks out the window.
All is present.
The shadows of the past
fall elsewhere.

This is the wilderness
she thinks.

And our tongues have become
dry   the wilderness has
dried out our tongues   and
we have forgotten speech.

She looks out the window.
All is present.

2. *Vider a mol*/Once again

Vider a mol
she tries to rise above circumstances.

Too much is at stake
this morning
yedn frimorgn
    every morning
to see what can be wrenched
from the unconscious
crowded darkness
fun ir zikorn
    of her memory.

It is there
di gantse geshikhte
fun folk
   the entire history
of the people.

Vider a mol
   she reaches out
and tries to hold on
clinging
   like a drowning
person
   to a flimsy plank.

Ober der yam iz groys
but the sea is vast
un di velt
   and the world
afile greser
   even larger
     afile greser.

3. *Zi flit*/She flies

Zi flit
vi a foygl
       like a bird
zi flit
ibern yam
        over the sea
iber di berg
         over the mountains.

Tsurik
     tsurik back
         back

zi flit
     and settles
oyf a boym
     on a tree
lebn a moyer
        near a wall

a moyer
fun a beys-oylem
        a wall
        of a cemetery.

4. *A beys-oylem*/A cemetery

Der moyer   the wall

oyf der zayt

     on this side

un oyf der zayt

     and on this side

oyf beyde zaytn   on both sides.

Oyf der zayt
a keyver

     on this side

a grave

     oyf der zayt
     a vistenish

on this side

     a wasteland.

Der moyer
a beys-oylem
oyf der zayt

     un oyf der zayt.

5. Kashes/Questions

In velkhn yor?

in what year?

Mit vemen?

with whom?

Di sibes?

the causes?

Der rezultat?

the outcome?

di geshikhte

the history

fun der milkhome

of the war

fun dem sholem

of the peace

fun di lebn geblibene

of the survivors

tsvishn fremde

among strangers

oyf der zayt

on this side

tsvishn meysim

among ghosts

oyf der zayt

on this side.

6. *Zi shemt zihk*/She is ashamed

Zi shemt zikh.
>> She has forgotten
>> *alts fargesn*
> forgotten it all.

>> Whom can I speak to?
>> she wonders.

di mame	the mother
der tate	the father
di bobe	the grandmother
der zeyde	the grandfather
di oves	the ancestors

alts
alts fargesn
forgotten it all

>> *di gantse mishpokhe*
>> the entire family

dos folk
the people.

> *Mit vemen*
> *ken ikh redn?*
> Whom can I speak to?

di meysim farshteyen
mir afile nit
>> even the ghosts
>> do not understand me.

7. *In der fremd*/Among strangers

Vi azoy?   how
she wonders
should I speak?

          Velkhe verter
which words
should I use
in der fremd

          among strangers?

Zog
bloyz dem emes

          speak
          only the truth
kayn lign nit

          no lies.

Zi gedenkt
She remembers
di lektsyes

          the lessons
di printsipn

          the principles

          un zi shvaygt

and she remains

          silent.

8. *Di tsung*/The tongue

Zi shvaygt.

Di verter feln ir
she lacks the words
and all that she can force

is sound
unformed sound:

a
der klang
        the sound

o
dos vort
        the word

u
di tsung
        the tongue

o
dos loshn
        the language

e
di trern
        the tears.

9. *Di rayze aheym*/The journey home

Zi flit
> she flies

vi a foygl
> like a bird

vi a mes
> like a ghost.

Zi flit
iber di berg
> over the mountains

ibern yam
> over the sea.

Tsurik
    tsurik back
>   back.

In der fremd
> among strangers

iz ir heym
> is her home.

    Do
here
ot do

> right here

muz zi lebn
> she must live.

Ire zikhroynes
> her memories
> will become monuments

ire zikhroynes
will cast shadows.

Etlekhe verter oyf mame-loshn/
A few words in the mother tongue

lemoshl: for example

di kurve   the whore
a woman who acknowledges her passions

di yidene   the Jewess   the Jewish woman
ignorant   overbearing
let's face it: every woman is one

di yente   the gossip   the busybody
who knows what's what
and is never caught off guard

di lezbianke   the one with
a roommate   though we never used
the word

dos vaybl   the wife
or the little woman

....

in der heym   at home
where she does everything to keep
yidishkayt alive

yidishkayt   a way of being
Jewish   always arguable

in mark   where she buys
di kartofl un khale
(yes, potatoes and challah)

di kartofl the material counter-
part of *yidishkayt*

mit tsibeles with onions
that bring *trern tsu di oygn*
tears to her eyes   when she sees
how little it all is
veyniker un veyniker
less and less

di khale   braided
vi ir hor far der khasene
like her hair before the wedding
when she was *aza sheyn meydl*
such a pretty girl

di lange shvartse hor
the long black hair
di lange shvartse hor

....

a froy kholmt   a woman
dreams *ir ort oyf der velt*
her place in this world
un zi hot moyre and she is afraid
so afraid of the words

kurve
yidene
yente
lezbianke
vaybl

zi kholmt   she dreams
un zi hot moyre   and she is afraid
ir ort
di velt
di heym
der mark

a meydl kholmt
a kurve kholmt
a yidene kholmt
a yente kholmt
a lezbianke kholmt

a vaybl kholmt
di kartofl
di khale

yidishkayt

zi kholmt
di hor
di lange shvartse hor

zi kholmt
zi kholmt
zi kholmt

Fradel Schtok

Yiddish writer. Born in 1890 in Skale, Galicia. Emigrated to New York in 1907. Became known when she introduced the sonnet form into Yiddish poetry. Author of *Erzeylungen* (Stories) in 1919, a collection in Yiddish. In 1927 switched to English and published a novel, *For Musicians Only*. Institutionalized and died in a sanitarium around 1930.

Language is the only homeland.
CZESLAW MIŁOSZ

They make it sound easy: some disjointed
sentences   a few allusions to
mankind.   But for me   it was not
so simple   more like   trying
to cover the distance   from here
to the corner   or between two sounds.

Think of it: *heym*   and   *home* the meaning
the same   of course   exactly
but the shift   in vowel   was the ocean
in which I drowned.

I tried. I did   try.
First held with Yiddish   but you
know it's hard. You write   *gas*
and   *street* echoes back
No resonance.   And — let's face it —
memory falters.
You try to keep track of the difference
like *got* and *god*   or *hoyz* and *house*
but they blur   and you start using
alley   when your mean *gesele*   or *avenue*
when it's a *bulevar.*

And before you know it
you're on   some alien path
standing before a brick house
the doorframe   slightly familiar.
Still   you can't place it
exactly. Passersby   stop.
Concerned   they speak   but you've
heard all this   before   the vowels
shifting   up and down   the subtle
change   in the guttural sounds
and now   it's nothing more
nothing   more   than   babble.
And so   you accept it.
You're lost. This time   you really
don't know   where you are.

Land or sea   the house floats before you.
Perhaps you once sat   at that window
and it was home   and looked out
on that *street* or *gesele*. Perhaps
it was a dead end   perhaps a shortcut.
Perhaps not.
A movement by the door.   They stand there
beckoning   mouths open and close:
Come in! Come in! I understood   it was
a welcome.   *A dank! A dank!*
I said   till I heard the lock
snap   behind me.

Der mames shabosim/My Mother's Sabbath Days

Inspired by Vella Grade in Chaim Grade's memoir

Bay undz iz es geven andersh.   I knew nothing
of the 613 *mitsves*   which did not bind me   nor
of the 3 which did   though I am sure my grandmother
Rikla Perczykow   knew them all   and I have a vague
image   of her covering her eyes   and swaying.

Shoshana   Róźka   Lodzia   Mamma Lo   and more recently
Rose   in short: my mother   in all her reincarnations
did not pass on   such things.
She'd given them up   even before she'd ever claimed them.
She was more modern   and besides   there were other matters
to teach   so by age 11   *kh'bin shoyn geven a brenendike sotsyalistke*
I was a passionate socialist   impatient   so impatient
to grow   into my knowledge   never guessing
there was no choice   for work   and rest   wrestled
in every human life   with work   inevitably
the unbeatable winner.

So for us it was different.   *Erev shabes*   was plain   *fraytik*
or more precisely: *piątek*   I remember   summer evenings
I'd wait for her   at the Mosholu stop of the Lexington Line.
Bright heat and light   at 6 o'clock.   She was full
of tales   of Miss Kant   the designer   a career woman
longing for home and family   in love with a handsome pilot
of Scottie   the model   who married smart   a wealthy buyer
and now sat brazenly chic   in a reform synagogue.
I listened   eager   to understand these   widow tales   of romance
amid the rush   of each season's showing   and once   even
saw   on a page of the *Times*   a mannequin   dressed in
the very gown   Mamma Lo had made.

All the way up Jerome Avenue   we'd walk   past the Jewish deli
where we never ate   (what was the point if you could make it at home?)
past the pizza place   where occasionally while shopping she'd buy me
a slice   past the outdoor groceries fruit stands   fabric   shoes
lingerie   and stationery stores — till Gun Hill Road   and Jade Gardens.
Perhaps I knew it was *treyf*.   She certainly did
but was not concerned.   We'd order   the salty wonton soup
chow mein   or pepper steak   and though she mocked the food
she never resisted.

It was Friday.   The shop was closed. We'd eat dinner and like the rich
lean leisurely back in our booth.   I didn't know it was *erev shabes*.
Still — she rested.

'67 Remembered

for Khane

In '67 you visited with your sister.
I was in Chicago.   Richard Speck had just murdered
seven nurses.   We were scared.   The war was only
a few days over   and everyone said
how well you and Gitl looked.   Who would
have thought   you'd just come
from a war-torn country
dressed chic   in late '60s fashion
smiling   easy   relaxed
confident   the worst was over?
I still have the photographs.

How different   that war
from that other   in your life:
Siberia   the Germans at your heels
your father chopping trees in the forest.
You learned Russian in the street
spoke Yiddish at home   wrote Polish
in the segregated schools.   You were
a linguist at eight   ready to master
even more tongues   for the sake of survival.

But in '67   you'd already mastered
it all.   You were so relaxed   so easy.
It was a joke   this war   despite
the casualties.   It was a joke
how relaxed   you were.

And wasn't I too?   Weren't we all?
Didn't we all glow from it
our sense of power finally achieved?
The quickness of the action
the Biblical routes
and how we laughed over
Egyptian shoes in the sand
how we laughed at another people's fear
as if fear was alien
as if we had known safety   all our lives.

And the Bank?
I don't remember   it mentioned
by any of us.
We were in Chicago — it was hard to imagine.
But twenty years later
I hear how they picked up what they could
placed it on their backs
how they marched through the hills
sparse   coarse grass   pink and yellow flowers
rough rocks   defying cultivation
how they carried   clumsy packs
clothing   utensils   images of a home
they might   never see again.
A sabra told me   who watched
their leaving as she sat safe
in an army jeep: it looked no different
than the newsreels at school
of French   Belgian roads.   It was simple
she said: people were fleeing   and
we egged them on.

Time passes.   Everything changes.
We see things differently.
In '67 you had not married yet   and we all
wondered why   never worrying about
marriage laws   or rabbinic power.

And now more than 20 years later
you live in Jerusalem   ruling
from your lacquered kitchen   and sit
in that dream house   trapped:
enough food   in your mouth
in your children's   and enough warm things
for winter (coats   shoes   woolen stockings
good for Siberia)
and there's no way out   no one to call
about a bad marriage.   It's simple:
a woman   without bruises
your lawyer says   there's not much hope
and you accept it:
I can't say I'm happy   but
I've got a truce.

Things fester.   We compromise.
We wake up   take new positions
to suit new visions   failed dreams.
We change.   Power does not so much corrupt
as blur the edges
so we no longer feel   the raw fear
that pounds in the hearts
of those trapped   and helpless.
In '67 in Chicago   we thought we'd be safe
locking the windows   till Speck was caught.
We did not know   there was a danger
in us as well   that we must remain vigilant
and open   not to power
but to peace.

Warsaw, 1983: *Umschlagplatz*

Ikh bin nisht geven in Treblinka.
I was never in Treblinka.
H. LEIVIK

No horrors this time.
It's 1983. June.   Summer.
Warsaw is tense   but over *Solidarność*
over amnesty.

A small white brick wall.
Two plaques in Polish   and Yiddish
to the effect   that from here
zaynen zey geforn kayn Treblinke.
Two stubby candles on either side
neither burning.   The guide
lights one with a lighter.
The wind blows it out.

A gas station pumping gas
right behind.   A building on
one side.   Perhaps   from that time
efsher an eydes.   Maybe it saw.
And there are tracks
I think.

I do not cry.   What's to cry
about?   An ordinary street.
People   going about
their business forty years later
tense about amnesty.

This street might have been my home.
This street might have been the beginning
of my journey to death.
I must remember:
it was neither.

I live on another continent.
It is 1983.   I am now a visitor.
History stops for no one.

East Jerusalem, 1987: *Bet Shalom* (House of Peace)

To a Palestinian woman whom I am afraid to name

Whether we like it or not
we must sit here.   What we feel
does not matter.   We are the heirs:
our legacy is in the air we breathe
the ground we stand on.

One of us lives   in the neighborhood
you were raised in
where you took   your first steps
and met the world.
Then everyone left.
Your uncles and aunts
carried their belongings
and left.   It was '48.

You ask us:
>   *Do you understand   can you imagine*
>   *what it must feel like to me?*
>   *To all of us?*
>   *I do not go back to those neighborhoods.*
>   *I just don't feel right.*
>   *Do you understand*
>   *what it means to all of us?*

We understand   we remember history
and understand it all:
the need for safety a safety
no one else can take away.
The need for control
not waiting in line   to get attention
or for the consciences of others to awaken.
We understand what it means to have children
who die   children who live and learn to be proud
of who they are.

Doubts   break through.
This is in the air   the reluctance
to have understanding be enough.
We ask: didn't you omit
part of the picture
didn't you leave out a piece   along the border
a piece of the sky   the very peak of a mountain
the bus bombed   the children in the schoolhouse
peaceful farmers   ploughing fields—
you left out part of the picture.

Understanding wraps us again   tightly
towards each other.

We remember the camps: during   and after.
During: there was murder   and resistance
more murder   *and after*: there was determination
sneaking in at night no lights burning
the small boats   the landings on the beach
when everyone else had said: don't go there
or there or there   or who wants them anyway
they've always been trouble   *and again after*:
bombings   massacres
we understand   the actions of a desperate people.

Doubts break us apart
we can barely breathe.   We ask:
why are you our problem too?   We can hardly hold
our own.   Why can't you just blend in
with your own kind?

Whether we like it   or not
we must sit here   and this is in the air.
You say to us:
    You must understand
    how it is for me.
    You are writers.
    Write about it.
You mean: Our voices carry.
Yours alone does not.

All of us part.   You move off   in a separate
direction.   The rest of us return
to the other Jerusalem.   It is night.

I still hear your voice.   It is in the air
now   with everything else   except sharper
clearer.   I think of your relatives
your uncles and aunts   I see the familiar
battered suitcases   cartons with strings
stuffed pillowcases
children sitting on people's shoulders
children running to keep up.

Always   there is migration
on this restless planet   everywhere
there is displacement   somewhere
someone is always telling   someone else
to move on   to go elsewhere.

Night.   Jerusalem.   *Yerushalayim.*
Jerusalem.   If I forget thee
Oh Jerusalem Jerusalem   Hebron
Ramallah   Nablus   Qattana   if I
forget thee oh Jerusalem
Oh Hebron   may I forget
my own past   my pain
the depth of my sorrows.

Her Birth
and Later Years

$(1991–2021)$

Footnotes

March 1939: Warsaw, Poland

In 2016, I was made aware of the existence of my father's student file in the archives of the Warsaw Polytechnic, the engineering school he attended before the war. It was miraculous that it survived given that so many other files were lost. Michał Klepfisz's file contained a signed original photograph (his ID), copies of his birth certificate, school transcripts, and his handwritten requests for financial aid. It was an incredible discovery to make at the age of 75, for until then my only physical connection to my father were two photographs, one when he was around 18 (a copy of the ID) and one when he was 8. Michał's last handwritten note was dated three weeks before his 26th birthday, just four years before he was killed.

I understand nothing   but the date
March 27   1939

I want to whisper:
      grab everyone   and run to the nearest port
         the nearest border

But he is worried   about tuition

He understands:
      oppression   hatred
         slavery   torture
but extermination? genocide? gas? ovens?
     Jakob   Myriam
       Gina   and Rikla?
all his Bundist comrades?
fellow students   athletes?
and
       Frydrych?

                    extermination?

I press:
forget the silverware   Babcia's lace   forget the books
the photo albums   the anniversary brooch   forget
the diplomas Jakob's   Myriam's   Gina's   yours
Majus's drawings   just tell Różka   to hurry
and get her mother   no time
for goodbyes   to Guta   Krysia   Majus
        but take the papers   money
in the desk   forget the protractor   rulers
pencils   notebooks   take the knapsacks
pack   scissors
clothes for   layers   hats   scarves
                a compass
remember   needle and thread   and also string
an extra pair of shoes
                Talk calmly   but hurry the old ones
Go!   run   don't look back   just *Go!* *Go!*

Michał:
        Don't try to be a hero   be my father
It's March   1939   in just 5 months
        the butcher   will begin   grinding meat

Warsaw, 1941: The story of her birth

i

but the father whispered
    that the doctors whispered
    choose one   choose *now*
        too long
        three days too long
        so kill it
        kill it   oh too long

and the doctors were ready   set
and the father was ready   set
    but   the mother didn't die
    and it   just wouldn't die
    (to spite them all   inside and out)
    and   not very much later
    the mother whispered:
    look how ugly it is   the head all squeezed
    so squashed
    its face so scratched   so   oh so ugly
    and does it have 10 fingers?
    and does it have 10 toes?

ii

but then   the father changed
        so changed   oh so changed
        and began to love it
        and how he loved it   so so so much
that he let it sit on his shoulders
        and ducked   ducked down
        as he walked through the doorway
        and it would laugh   laugh
        so high
                    so high

iii

imagine: *babcia* and *dziadek*
       cluck   how clever she is
       watch   how she sits
       on the floor   in the kitchen
       so content   and pulls the potatoes
       from the dirty sack
       one   one   one   at a time
       almost like counting
       look how busy she is   oh so so so clever
       taki cud   this miracle of a child
       how lucky to have it
             szczęście

a nes   shhhhhh   *a nes*

       and the days   passed

iv

and then   the potatoes were gone
and there was only the street
      there was noise   and there was quiet
         and the aunt or friend or someone
         not the father and   not the mother
     who would do such a terrible thing
     and leave her   there on the street
     in the noise   and the quiet?
         today no one knows the name or spot
         and who could find it anyway
         with everything gone
     everyone gone   and what had it done?
     what had it done?   to be left
     standing and crying   as they watched

and then a woman   or nun
     found her   and took her away
     with other found children
and i've heard that she cried   for a long time

     she cried how she cried
     with no *tatuś*   no *mama*   no *babcia* or *dziadek*
     with only the nuns   grim lipped
     who inspected   for germs
     watched her   and her
     and the sick children   rocking
     and banging   their heads against the bars
     who cried   and cried
     and how she cried   with them
     and how she cried

and i was told   how he once came
        and said he had chocolate
        brought chocolate for her   just for her
        only for her   whom he had wanted to kill
        and who had sat on his shoulders
        so high   oh so high
        and now said: i have brought   chocolate
        just for her   only for her
        and how the nun   black habit   and dry thin lips
        said: if you come   again   i'll put it out
        on the street   on the street   i'll put it out
                into the noise   and quiet

so he never came again
        and *babcia* and *dziadek*
        they were taken
        and the aunt   she died
        in a hospital bed
        and later   on a rooftop
        he   was shot
                he was killed

        he died

        and that was that

        and that was that

vi

and eventually the mother came and got her
and i heard   they both survived

but that's a very different matter
        (though not unrelated)
        as to how she was born
        and how he had said
        kill it   kill it
        and how   she was stubborn
        and wouldn't die

Pesakh: Reynolda Gardens, Winston-Salem

for my mother, Rose Perczykow Klepfisz

1. Winter

This spring   as the weeping cherries burst
torrential   with pale tears
urging me towards   harmony and hope

I sit remembering how   you and I
had walked here   on a February day
relishing the sun in late winter warmth
certain of spring and its inevitable hope
imagining   its blossoming.

A few narcissus   had already revealed their passion
the dark green leaves   stark against the dull earth
but mostly   the grounds were empty   like the desert
        stiff stems   bare hedges   trees like sticks
        all promise   in which we both believed.

2. Spring

Now   the promise is fulfilled
spring is lush again.   But I had not foreseen
nor understood   how the desert blooms only in its oases
leaving the remains   barren and brown dry.

This *pesakh*   you call and cry:
"*I am alone*"   and count your years
backwards and forwards.   More than eighty back
you watched death   gouge and eat   your family
your friends   your life
                    and then spit them out in a footnote
among   history's scraps.

You know that   tonight those who are left
drink wine   break the crumbling *matses*
and count their blood   drop by drop by drop.

Their seder tables   are heavy with blood.
Children   of children of children   stammer   the story:
they speak   the desert language of blood
forget   there is a language of water.

3. The seder table

The Egyptians drowned in the Red Sea
for their blood   was alien   as their beliefs.
And you   neither blood   nor Jewish stranger
are now Egyptian   weeping tears
as you prepare for sleep alone in alien disbelief.

I have learned a bitter lesson   of
bonded blood   around the seder table:
this is where it starts
                    the division between the blood of ours
                                              and the water of theirs
this is where it starts:
the division between   mine and not-mine
where wars begin and end   and restart again
declaring this blood   that water.

You believed there would   always be a seder
waiting for you   when we were all safe
but learned   so late   there are mirages
and   while some get seated
others   left behind   drown in the desert sand.

Mitsrayim: Goat Dream

1.

i stayed in that narrow place
        slavery and all
it was home   i didn't hate
them

        not even the bricks

later   i heard
about the parting waters

2.

in the dream
my chest   is bleeding
as i wake from unconsciousness
on a gritty   sandy shore

i have been beaten
i have been raped

the goat is dead   but
i do not know which corpse
is hers   so many heads protruding
from the sand

i remember   her body
soft and warm
when i put my arms   around her
heard her bleating   felt her beating heart
as we slept and dreamed   in the straw

3.

in the dream
it now happens   i'm in the town
where   i am meant   to meet them
the people who   need to hear   what i lived through

but   no one listens
or they're distracted
by important travel plans
        sights to marvel at
                so many wonders   to recall

now   i see
the goats   are gone
and   no one wants
to pass on   the memory
of this country
        its miracles
        its pyramids
                and all the wanderers
                looking for home

Der soyne/The Enemy: An Interview in Gaza

i.

I live here with my family.
The Jews come. I throw rocks.
I yell out: *Heil Hitler!*
My friend is shot with a rubber bullet.
They take him to the hospital. He will
live but he's a cripple.

My mother weeps: When will it end?
Me? I'm happy school is closed.
Who needs to study?
I like to see them hide
behind the walls. Down with the Jews!
Long live Palestine!

ii.

Ikh voyn do mit der mishpokhe.
Di yidn kumen. Ikh varf shteyner.
Ikh shray: Heil Hitler!
A khaver vet geshosn mit a gumener koyl.
Men nemt im in shpitol. Er vet
lebn ober er vet zayn a kalike.

Di mame veynt: ven vet es zikh endikn?
Ikh? Ikh bin tsefridn az di shul iz farmakht.
Vos darf ikh lernen?
'Sgefelt mir ven zey bahaltn zikh
unter di vent. Nider mit di yidn!
Zol lebn palestine!

In memory of Razan al-Najjar

Razan al-Najjar, a 21-year-old woman identified as a nurse, was killed on June 1, 2018, during one of the numerous confrontations occurring at the time on the Gaza border between Palestinian protestors and Israeli soldiers.

i

to be honest
I really am not sure how to pronounce her name
but I know who she was
and know she was 21

there are international disagreements
        was it intentional
        was it an accident
        was she helping the wounded
or was she resisting
[meaning: deliberately throwing ... what? ... at those rifles and tanks]

do we feel glad
do we feel guilty and outraged

do we feel safer
do we feel defensive

meaning   protective
of ourselves   we are in danger
after all   we are at war

is she a martyr
is this exactly what Hamas had hoped for
or is this
     [please remember the antecedent
     a dead 21-year-old nurse]
simply a   PR nightmare
for Jews   in and out of Israel
that must be addressed   in international media

ii

if we save one life
we save the world

if we destroy one life
do we destroy the world

Is the world destroyed
because Razan al-Najjar
was shot   accidentally

or is the world   better off
with this 21 year old dead

if destroyed
are we destroyed with it [the world]
with her [Razan Al-Najjar]

iii

I marvel: isn't it incredible
that we are arguing over
the death of a 21-year-old nurse
Razan Al-Najjar
by a bullet
aimed   ricocheted
or bounced off

from this one   a sniper   or from another
also a 21 year old   inexperienced and frightened
or that one   a fighter for his people and nation
or that one who didn't know how to get out of the service
or this one who wanted to prove that she too   was brave

isn't it incredible?

Instructions of the dying elder to his successor concerning monuments, memorials, museums, and other architecturally uplifting structures

Inspired by the Israeli government's announcement of plans to build a Museum of Tolerance in Jerusalem on part of the site of The Mamilla Cemetery, a Muslim cemetery reputed to go back to the 7th century.

These laws are hacked:
    on rocks in comets' tails
    passing slowly across our bent time and space
They are chiseled:
    on tablets buried in seas
    flush with iridescent fish or
    turgid with oil   and civilization's dregs
They are inked in black   sometimes embossed in gold
    in Egyptian hieroglyphs   Farsi scripts
        a monk's Latin tome

Thus   it has always been:
    the graves of ancestors of strangers of neighbors
and of   no ones
    ours   theirs   mine   yours
    are never to be disturbed

For on each gravesite   the soil has been mulched
    with human soul and bone
    with tears of mourners
    this air   ash   and   salt of comet showers
    must never be disturbed

Understand further: such ground   is   forever sacred
not for a god   but for ourselves
remember: we may not build   indifferent to the dead
houses   monuments   not even our lives

So weigh carefully   whether today's new   is necessary
and make that decision wisely
balancing action   against the weight of stone
There's just so much space   so much earth

And if you must   then erect your marble monuments   museums   to your better self
elsewhere
            (but   may i suggest: perhaps
        not at all)

Keep the past holy   Be fair   above all   to those not visible
Always be kind   and   of course   generous
especially generous   in uncertain chaotic times
Do not take for yourself   what you would not give
to others   and do not add   even more upheavals
                                                    to this volcanic earth

Look: here was a stone   once carried   ground   glazed by glaciers
millennia past   then carved by a father   millennia later   to cover the sack of his stillborn
child   who never breathed   the chilled air outside her mother's womb   or laughed
or cried   or sucked   or smiled or made anyone   happy   even for the briefest moment

But day after day   the father   carved her name
so the child   would be known   to her family   her clan
and could lie   among them   safe

The rock is almost gone   sunk into the ground
the hemp sack   long rotted into the earth
and the parents' sadness   is as invisible today
as the soul of the stillborn was at birth   all we see is
a nub   a crumbling corner   pressing silently through
ordinary grass   yet must we not honor him   her
that family's grief?

Remember: yours   will certainly become   theirs
              (and i may add: eventually no one's)
                    it's a historical law   don't count on skipping
                    generations
              instead   keep looking to the sky
              and to the soil   and try to understand your place between here
and there

Remember also: Monuments aim to expiate   (though i've always believed
they try to sneak us
                                   past our sins)
but never do

Your tolerance   requires no plot   no grand design
surely   no land   It only needs
the open air   where outstretched arms   in one embrace
enfold   the wrenching grief of death   and the comfort of
undisturbed eternity

Dearest Friend: Regarding Esther Frumkin

Esther Frumkin (1880–1943): Passionate Yiddishist, Bundist, Kombundist, leader of *Yevsektsiya* (Jewish division of the Communist Party), editor of *Emes* (Truth), died in the Gulag.

I miss the children terribly
their nonsense   the silky skin
of their arms and fingers   still unhardened
by play or exploration   the baby's fin-like
gestures (is he still swimming or has he
finally accepted air and the downward pull of gravity?)

I'm in that phase again: regret at what I
didn't do   couldn't do and did
feeling victimized   that some decisions were
made more by time and others   than by me.
I know I'm wrong: it's nonsense   and it'll pass.
Meantime   it would be good
to see you   to rehash things

                              again.

Am still mulling over Esther   her choices
and what she must have felt   hearing that last verdict
betrayed by the very revolution   the government
she helped forge   what she felt
hearing former friends   testify and concur:
not death but a deserved exile

                              again.

What did she think   watching the country   through the train window
chained   and exhausted   three decades after those
earlier convictions?   Did she have regrets   could she pinpoint
the moments   of her strategic mistakes   review
whom she ignored?   willfully excluded?   carelessly put down?
Or did she think she was blameless?   always principled?
Or better yet, did she continue believing   they'd see their mistake
that eventually   it would all   be turned around
and she'd return   to the necessary   radical work?
Whom did she want to save?   whom did she relegate
to an uninhabitable   swamp?
I wish I could   probe   her self-awareness:
her grasp of what   she had done
what she'd   left behind   for historians to parse.

I understand it all so much better now than I would have
twenty years ago.   Politics to succeed   must
act   with unquestioned certainty.   Poetry on the other hand
is another matter   passion of certainty   of course
but inevitably   mixed   with all our aching doubts
and failings: we need   both to continue
but at what cost   with each.

I keep wondering   what she   would have thought
watching the statues   falling to the ground
watching   Lenin's lips   press against the Russian   Georgian
soils   before his head was melted down
for artists   to reform.
Think of the spectacle: a mile-long line
for Moscow's first McDonalds   or
Washington diplomats and Wall Street investors
their suits unwrinkled despite the lengthy flight
emerging from the airplanes   to Russian military music   and
stepping lively   on the readied   red carpet.
Would that spectacle   have revitalized
her revolutionary fervor: "I and they   may have been wrong,
but then again . . . the revolution itself was right."

These   are peculiar   sad   conflicting times.
I know it'll congeal   the contours will emerge. There's always
risk   in dedicating oneself to the present.   Did Esther know that?
But really   what option do we have? to just sit   pure   and watch?

Write soon. Come visit. I want especially to show you
the unconquerable roses.   They give me strength and hope.
They bloom   no matter what.
Kiss the children. Write   write   but come soon.

Millet's *Flight of Crows*

Five ways to view a drawing

1. The artist draws it almost like the Trinity:
The girl [woman?] is placed in the middle   holding the rope
[her power?] which keeps the cows close to her on either side

Note: the irreverence.   He presents her with her back to us.
One cow's rear   faces the viewers [us]   drawn
on the same plane   as the other cow's head.
Food and dung   interchangeable   the artist seems to say.
Both animals   appropriately look to the ground
for nourishment.   But we know   the cows are her food
that is: they provide milk to drink or sell   or churn.

For the moment, the briefest moment [the moment of this drawing?]
the girl's needs are being taken care of.   While the cows graze   she is free
to gaze [upward] towards the birds and sky.

          Q: Is it significant   that it is crows that evoke her deepest longing?
          Q: Had the artist not told us   would we have known
what birds had suddenly   flapped   out of that sparse grove?
[Note: he simply draws; it is we who decide if the grove is sparse or thin.]

Let us go back.

2.   The figure: There is no way for us to know if she's a young girl
or a worn-out woman.   The artist has placed her almost squarely
with her back to us. We see only the thick rounded line of profile [cheek].
We see only the dress   the carefully [modestly?] covered head. Nothing about her is loose
or exposed.   No wisp of hair   no blouse or shirt slipping from the waist. He draws her
self- contained   compact   filling the precise   space   she has been assigned.

     Q: Regarding her power: Is the distance to the crows   an expression
       of hope
    untested   or an expression   of long unrecognized   unfulfilled desire?

Let us look more closely.

3.   The void: There is another space   which we should make note of:
the void between desire   and execution a void which we must
    conclude neither girl
nor crone   can breach.
The artist is careful in his composition of this moment:
          for whoever she is   this woman must understand
                    [now or later]
that flight was never meant for her   that her centrality
will keep her as firmly rooted to the ground   as the distant trees
as the grazing cows.

4. The dress: perhaps a substitute for the face. In this predominantly brown
and muted drawing   [on blue-gray paper]
we see a sliver [swash?] of blue   on the long skirt
a blue occasionally echoed   in the surrounding field.

This blue   perhaps reflects   her romantic version   of a sky
she dreams of   since the artist   is unequivocal   in the sky
he presents to her [and us]: gray and lined   and in places   a mirror image
    of the trees   their branches.

And of course for the birds   the sky   is always sky   gray   blue or indifferent: the birds
soar.

5. The light: it's brightest at the horizon and makes it seem
the crows   are flying   into dark clouds that in turn
appear to be [in part at least]   extensions of the tops   of trees.
This technique   is echoed in the topmost branches
and uppermost   sky   as if wood could transform itself
and   become air.

No such possibility or fantasy is reflected in the foreground. The human figure
and the cows   are distinctly themselves
[no hope of blending or transformation here] and none are silhouetted against
the sky.

Instead all three   are drawn standing   well below   the horizon
against the backdrop   of the monotonous field
and in stark contrast to the animals   though her head   is raised upward
this woman [girl] remains   far beneath   the distant light
tethered forever
to this earth.

Mourning Cycle

Parsing the question

forget the common words
and answer instead:

I found a dead mouse
under the cabinet   stiff and
curled   in a fetal position

the flowers   in the vase
are now   powder   dusting
the books in the bookcase

where the bed   stood
two chairs   face each other
ready for conversation

the candles   stand   unlit
by   the box of matches

a new mystery on tv

when I turn the key
I hold my breath:

> will King Rat be at the table
> banging   for his portion
> of cheese?

sometimes   I too   sit down
and bang   for my cheese

sometimes   I turn on the tv
open another   book

often   I lie down   and tell myself
this is a nightmare:
> I will wake up

This House

After four years   I return to
this peace
this empty space
with its paint spattered floor
grateful   that you let me in
when you were so afraid
another presence   would overwhelm it.

There are so many ghosts
you would be   sad:
Dave's Mini Market is gone
so is the Country Store
also   the grocery   in the next town
though the bagel place   keeps on
across the road   from the Sunday   flea market.

I drove on the back road   it's paved now
almost didn't recognize
that hunting lodge   four walls with a roof
and now   a live-in house
that bicycle   dangling from the tree above
that silly pond: gone. The pig farmer's barn
is locked (remember those noisy little piglets
how he held them by their legs   so we could see them
up close?)   no trace of them   so freshly pink
running nowhere   down the dirt path.
And the woman with the goats
she's gone   too
as is the flaming lavender trailer   where two women
lived   and we never did   get beyond
our own suspicions   for whom could we have asked?

You knew the name   of every   insignificant road
at every turn   and I am trying to remember your routes
and stop now at the place where   you wanted
me   to cut some   purple flowers   still wild blooming on a bank.
Today I placed a few   in that small green vase.

The truth: the house needs mending
so long neglected   it needs your care.

I'm trying   to channel you
repairing   clapboards
the broken well cover   the broken steps.

You may be gone   but are always
with me: we're two ghosts joined

and when I clear the roses   when I cut
the strangling vines   I can hear you whisper:
          go help   the privets
          let the privets
                              breathe.

Liberation of the roses

You'd think   they'd put up   more resistance
being transplanted   from the dunes   hardy   to be sure
but it's been   four years   and now   they're almost invisible
tied up   by wiry weeds   with determined stalks
four years   with no help   from the outside
all tangled   and strangled
a surprise   that any survived at all
(snails   also having taken over
indifferent to   rose or stubborn   weed).

I pull
and the weeds   cave.

I remember it   as if I'd done it
just last spring   and not four years ago
late   afternoon   when the roots had loosened
their grip   on the powdered dirt
while you collected   broken branches
in the green wheelbarrow   anxiously
cleaning up   winter's debris.

The first few days   during spring's return
you'd barely speak   so busy   and excited
with everything that   needed tending
drying out the well   examining the paint
a cracked step   a hole   burrowed into the barn wall.

I hardly paid attention   though
I must have noticed   for I'm doing   exactly
what you'd have done   cared for   the house
following your instructions
liberating   the roses
and working   off my own instinct
just as I did
when I   cared   for you.

trees

he remembers   when they were
merely twigs   and he a boy
and now   more than 40 years later
they tower   over the house

unlike us   they age elegantly
lush   and proud   oh so   proud
there's no   timidity there
they hold   their ground

they can and do   outlive us all
you're gone   and can't even bear
witness   to their resilience

i'd like to believe   that you live
on through them   i'd like to believe
that they make   me less lonely
less mournful   in your absence

but i don't

i can only acknowledge
you once planted them
nurtured them   worried over them
the weight of   water   heavy snow
the hungry deer   gnawing their bark
the local vandals
the lack of rain

they survived
you couldn't

wound: a memory

her heart has   failed
and so have her kidneys

but she's   panicked   over
a small scratch   above her right wrist
and sits on the edge of the bed   waiting for
"something to be done"

"blood"   she says   an edge
of hysteria   as she adds *"from my flesh"*

I propose   a plan
antibiotic gel   gauze   paper tape
and carefully   lightly   wind a fresh
white   bandage over the wound
and wrist

she examines   the dressing
pleased   by its purity
my earnestness   in the wound's care

she is   calm
lies down   to rest   comforted
that once again
she has been saved

Wind chime

It hangs on the deck rail
a small bright red   mobile
dangles   from its center.

It's a breach   I know   but I'm keeping an eye
on myself.   I won't plant a weeping willow
(your most despised: who wants to look
at a tree   that cries all day? you asked
I do   I answered   sniffling over my lost cause).

You did compromise   with the hawthorn
but it   never bloomed
much to our mutual   disappointment.
Still I had to save it from your
determined   doom. It spoiled   some line
for you   as you eyed   the meadow
from the deck's high   ground.
We stopped talking about it
but I knew   you would have cut it down
without sentiment   had I not been around.

This one   is barely audible (who am I
apologizing to?). The red   float
reminds me of the cardinal   you loved
to watch   and all those other birds
ravenous   clutching at your   feeders
suspended above the boxes of your summer flowers
so lush   luxurious   so dizzy.

It's small   quiet.

Grief changes   and doesn't

Trying to name what doesn't change
NAOMI SHAHIB NYE

i reassure: the pain   does change
it   moves   and the knife   so long in your back
when you come   home   is still   with you
                                but now it lies
withdrawn and sheathed
in a kitchen drawer   its edge
        dull   and worn

still   the loneliness   remains
            as sharp   and renewed
as   the mist at dawn   that   nothing
nothing   can protect   you from

it floats   through   the kitchen   the studio
        and is   everywhere
                                outside
it cocoons   you   soft
                brushes   fragile against your face

                        who touched me just now?
why no one
silence answers

and the rooms   are as hollow
as empty   as they were
when you   left.

Entering the stream

I had some fish

I took a deep breath

Then I drank   ice water
from a frosted glass
just as you did

Another deep breath

Then I walked outside   saw other people
hurrying   to their lives
everyone   seemingly late for something
and I wondered: am I also   late?

You're not with me
so perhaps I am too early?
                                          I want to stop
till you catch up
but still   an unseen current pulls   me in
further   and deeper

and late   each night
                              in darkness
I await   the next day's news

between shadow and night:
a treatise on loneliness

i.

between shadow and night
    the stars struggle
        against a dying sun

dawn flushes faint and unaware

a woman rises   out of the darkness
    shadow days greet her
    as she faces the sun

ii.

who'll tell her the truth
  about the coming days?
how the mementos   are already
    nothing
but dust
how the stone
  beneath her heart
      is now nothing but salt
rubbing the wound
again
again
before she sinks
into a dreamless   night

iii.

and who'll hear her truth
    about these present days?
how loneliness fills her aching mouth
    fills her belly   like the stale bread
    they fed her
    to keep her blood   flowing

who'll hear her truth?

iv.

between shadow   and night
the stars struggle
against a dying sun
opal   and   ruby

a woman writes in a book
flushed   unaware
of a woman   light years away
in a parallel   life
sated   and full

the woman who walked   barefoot   alone
the woman who   wandered away

v.

i will not tell you what you already know
the beggars working the cars each night
the tired workers   the drunks half-fallen
how the streets are filled with hunger   despair
the huddled men smoking   the children   bored   then abandoned
the man who sold the monkey clapping cymbals
the woman who did a jig halfway down the block
the boy   who shot himself   but did not die
and stared   strapped in a chair for the rest of his life

i will not tell you what you already know
how no one believed what they read or saw
how truth lost out   and then disappeared

vi.

instead i will whisper what you may have forgotten
a treatise on loneliness and unalterable facts

first the denial:
it can be overcome
like a steep staircase
that you need to climb
slowly so slowly
yet you'll reach the top
and view serenely the dizzying height

second the potion:
which can cure it all
in a regimen of days
never skip even one
and one morning you'll wake
relieved

and then there's the truth:
i'll never again feel
her hand on my thigh
reminding me of the boundary
between her life and mine

And Death Is Always with Us

For Jean Swallow: whom I barely knew

in memory of Jean Swallow
lesbian writer
September 8, 1953–January 16, 1995

Here's what you've missed (and it's only been two days):
    the earthquake in Japan
    the recovery in California (short-lived)
    the official declaration of war   on affirmative action
    my last letter   to you   with suggestions and questions.

Now   everyone feels guilty: if only I hadn't yelled
if only I had written sooner   if only I'd been
more welcoming   if only I'd given in
as if each of us   were responsible
and you a mere onlooker
a manipulated victim of your own suicide.

It's hard to imagine   anything less passive:
the repeated gestures
300 aspirins
swallowing handfuls   washing each down
then swallowing another   again   and again.

And yet your last letter   just a few days before
was full of   hope and the future: a novel
taking shape   each night
poetry shimmering   for the time being
on the back of a dream   both vague and solid.

Shortly before that
you were visiting New York and   you talked of a prose poem
rejected by some who had said: this is not
how a poem should look.
Where should the lines
end? you had asked   and then the eternal:
what *is* poetry   after all?

I replied the only thing I knew:
our poems are like our lives   sometimes
carefully crafted   but mostly haphazard
shaped by unleashed   instinctual needs
we barely recognize   much less understand.
A poem is totally your own   I advised. Stick by it.
Ignore what others say.

I remember that day's conversation.
We were walking aimlessly   oblivious of city streets
only vaguely concentrating on looking for your car
which you'd forgotten was parked: where?

I've talked poetry to others. Some barely listen.
Perhaps you   listened too hard
and shaped your poems   like a series
of bottles fitted to the palm of your hand.

But at the time: the talk seemed to bring
a breath of relief.   Yes you said,
I must   remember that.

Now I must remember:
        in the matter of suicide
nothing we do   we who go on living   matters much:
the postponed letter the unspoken wise advice.

You needed to die   didn't worry   what would
happen two days later   indifferent
to the difference between wraparound prose
and the cut off line.

And the rest of us
        lover   collaborator
        old friend   or   recent acquaintance
we choose to live on:
your suicide
neither guilty excuse   nor hard lesson
for the lives we lead
or may decide to take.

My mother at 99: Looking for home

Her eyes   tell me of her longing
to escape   her wheelchaired body
her mouth   can only moan.

Words have wandered off
locked up   in a backroom closet
lips pressed   tightly
she groans: *let me out!*
                    let me go home!

She means: that first home
the one   with candles   and no bath
the home of   too few beds
and hunger   but she insists   joy

with *bobe*   trying to keep peace
"Hit *me*!   Hit *me*!" she'd tell them   laughing
when things got out of hand
and each had insisted on being the winner.

"I was her favorite" she once whispered
with pride   and I wondered if I should
believe her.

Yes   there was a home   where she returned
late at night   after a day's work of sewing   and
an evening class   she was just 12
small for her age   dreaming only of   books
waiting to be read

she'd recite *Pan Tadeusz*   silently to herself
before   falling asleep   her favorite.

This apartment of forty-five years
that she so loved   and loved to show off
the balcony   the tree-filled views
is now an unmarked island   on a world map
its packed bookshelves line all the rooms   filled with stories
many with her name
                              gifts and givers
forgotten.

If she could just escape   this prison
abandon   this useless body
and return   to that first place
words   would also return and gather meaning
even Mickiewicz himself   would be there to proclaim
in passionate   perfect verse

        that home   is truly loved
        only   after it is lost   forever.

She cannot admit
this will not happen
that she's locked up for good
that there is no escape

and so she moans   in the wheelchair
her eyes begging
                        let me go! let me go!

"Mameshi   Mameshi"
my eyes tell her:

        "I am here. There is no key.
        But I promise   I promise
        I will come again."

my mother's loveseat

my mother's loveseat was velvet gold
   and years later I would wonder
if she'd ever had a lover or been resigned
     to time spent with just friends

she was widowed in hiding
   at 29
   when she couldn't cry
   or scream after she was told
so she learned to press her lips tight
to be hard and to stay numb

a survivor's loveseat
   is many things
     love lost and regretted
   love hoped for but never gained

a golden loveseat is a wished-for fairytale ending

when I saw it last
   my mother's loveseat stood
on the sidewalk waiting
   to be picked up

July 22: Geology

July 22, 1914—Warsaw, Poland
   Shoshana Perczykow is born

July 22, 1937 — Warsaw
   It is Shoshana's 23rd birthday
   Shoshana and Michał Klepfisz get married and go to Paris for their
      honeymoon
   He calls her Mała because he is tall and she is small

July 21, 1942—Warsaw Ghetto
   Mała is in the hospital, too weak to walk after goiter surgery
   Michał and his sister Gina stretch out their arms, entwine their hands,
      create a chair for Mała, and take her down the stairs (how many
      floors?) out of the hospital and to their parents' apartment

July 22, 1942—Warsaw Ghetto
   It is Mała's 28th birthday and 5th wedding anniversary
   She is in an apartment with Michał, Gina, Miryam, Jakob, Babcia Solomon
      and one-year-old Irenka
   The *Grossaktion* in the Warsaw Ghetto begins
   Between July 22 and September 1942, more than 250,000 Jews depart by train
      from the Warsaw Ghetto's *Umschlagplatz* for resettlement in Treblinka,
      75 miles from Warsaw
   No one knows exactly when Miryam, Jakob, Babcia Solomon died: before,
      during, or after the *Grossaktion*
   They only know about Michał and Gina
   Mała and Irenka are the only ones in that apartment who survive the war

July 22, 1943—Warsaw, Aryan Side
   Lodzia marks her 29th birthday, 6th wedding anniversary, and the first days of
      the 4th month of her widowhood

July 22, 2014—Bronx, New York
  Rose celebrates her 100th birthday
  No one mentions the other events—nor were they ever mentioned
    in all the years before

July 22, 2021—Brooklyn, New York
  Earlier in the year, Irena becomes confused and marks this day in her
    calendar:
        "Mameshi's 5th *yortsayt*"
  It is Shoshana's 107th birthday
  The day before, July 21, Irenka figures it out

Jamaica Wildlife Preserve:
September

She's not like these other two
(she tells herself):
slow   and overly careful women
aged and aging
shoes soled to the ground.

More like these birds
the mallard   goose
and swan
some nesting down for the winter
some preparing for flight.

More like a wild yellow flower
succulent cactus
brown autumn berry
food for birds
a wonder for the nature-starved visitor
obediently following
arrows and signs.

She stands apart
(she tells herself):
a stranger to the passion
that moves   them all
towards winter
a stranger   to the relation
between shore and   inevitable ice
to the meaning of   the Concord jet
soaring above Jamaica Bay
reaching London in record time.
She is startled at the simultaneous
start   of winter
and the undiminished light
the curve of bay grass
as it gives up and in
to a chilling wind and rising tide.

She'd always thought
death would be   violent
connected to metal or explosives
bones splintered   body torn apart
certainly not this silent diminishing
flesh within a shriveling skin
weakening always
in brilliant autumn light.

She's not like the others
(she tells herself):
but knows the weight
of self-deceit
in the aging   hardened heart
as she searches for birds
and counts:
three women ten twenty
thirty years apart
standing on the calm protected shore
watching the encroaching winter
watching each other   accept
the strength the pull
        of the undertow.

The old poet   reconsiders acting

For years it had been easy to play
the green-eyed rage and purple sorrow
dredge up   an orphan's accusing glance
or mouth   the widow's halting stance.

But now putting forth a dramatic face
or gesture   is no longer
within my reasoned reach: only what I am
can be: an aging ordinary woman
calm   along the ordinary street.

If words were acts I would have been
a mighty actor   played Sappho   Jane
Virginia in outrageous drag   replaced
Lev or Herman if they'd lost their place.
But a poet's words are but sound and paper
echoes and afterimages   of an unrecorded drama
which plays itself out with   or without
the poet's help.

Still I do remember the flowers of '46
the greening gooseberries   the rose-pink pears
tapered like breasts of self-conscious girls.
That year   I first felt   hardwood words
compounded   in my mouth held my pen
stiff   between the lines   did battle
with the runny ink   and dreamed
of magic golden penmanship stars.
Later when the house had joined itself with night
I'd rush   outside   beneath the moonless
dizzy sky   and blushing   devour blushing pears
tart gooseberries   on the sly.

Regret and rue are not the words I seek:
earth and magic come closer to it
the poet's need is to be rapt   and joyous
to soar.   I am amazed:
the strut the lines   the voice
are gone. Somewhere back there
I turned.   Perhaps it is time.
I've moved off the apron and now stand
silent   on the curtained stage.

The old poet   tries unsuccessfully to bring
chaos   back into her order

The old poet   takes her typewriter
out of the case   the one which handed
her the prize   and some local notoriety.
It still clacks   like the goose
that laid the golden egg   though today
it's sheer bravado.

Recent years   are but one long day
whose night   never darkens: Oh, let me
sleep   again   and let me wake
to a fresh and blinking sunrise.
But the day   drags on   year after
moonless year   an unbroken row of breakfasts
now with blueberries   now potatoes.
It's got to be a joke   she says
someone's brainless   practical joke.

Perhaps what's needed   is insemination
cross fertilization   to shake things up
some Neruda   Lorca   or maybe a whip line
from Dickinson   a dash of Sexton's wrath.
Something's got to give eventually   you'd think?

Everything they promised   did not come true:
not love   not peace   not earthly ease.
Only death   has proven faithful sticking close
passing the orange juice   scrambling the eggs
putting the typewriter   back   where it belongs.

The old poet   and Orion

It's validating to know he's as stuck
as I am   always looking to target
whatever comes along.
But I have noticed that nothing
nothing ever happens.   He's been standing
there   in the same position for as long
as I can remember.   I thought
it romantic   devoting one's life
to seizing   the perfect moment.
Tonight   I'm having   real doubts.

Still I try to be   encouraging
keeping a positive outlook   but
(is this familiar?)   he insists: "It's hopeless.
By the time   I see the winking goose
its studded tail   of galactic dust
bad news: it's dead   and black and even deadly
ready to eat me in the cosmic dark."

Now I'm in despair:
he's doubting his own existence
and mine (none of this is going the way
I'd planned).   So I strike back with paradox:
"Shadow" I call to him   "imploded being
empty space   with a few well placed stars
I know   to the bottom of my   cloven feet
that today   I am still the flesh   I was
when I was born   and that I stand here
vigilant with you   eye to eye   tracking all
that passes through: earth water   air
light years   of light."

The old poet's become   tired

The old poet's become
tired   of looking   for new ways
to say the same old   same old:

"Here's the poop:
We die. Period."

She's cranky   unpleasant
turned   her back on the plaguing questions:
"Spare me   Plato   and his empty cave
the old rabbinic debates   over the hereafter
the frantic judicial   injunctions against
the right-to-die and doctor assisted   suicide.
In the time remaining   let's just cut to the chase
admit   what a lifetime   of words   denied:
The sword is mightier   than the pen.
Read   the paper. And please
don't ask me to heal   and hope."

Her skin shrivels and flakes.
She knows   her options:
Regeneration's a thing of the past.
Every morning she swallows aspirin
to thin   her blood   against constrictions.
But she's got   her wits   about her:
She takes   it easy   and keeps
the blank page
                    blank.

The old poet remembers   the immigrant girl

From the start
the chorus always said:
We don't want what you have to give.
We don't care who you are.
You have to become different.   Change.

When she first walked into   class
and pledged   with the wrong hand
they all chorused. She stood mute
ashamed   as the teacher corrected her
still mute   when they chorused
the incomprehensible sounds.

After a time   she understood
that girls would talk   behind her back
about her ugly stockings   the bows in her hair
the braids too tightly braided.
It was all noise and dust and cars
and loneliness: a mother at work
a glass of milk   a sandwich waiting
on the kitchen table.

Everyone whispered.   She was no one's friend.
They locked her in a closet   until
her mother came home
and claimed her.   She learned
she would be outside   that people
would stop speaking to her   and not tell her
that there was always   a struggle
to be in   which meant that someone
always had to be out.

She was dressed in humiliation
the homemade skirts   by the mother who had
no husband.   Once in class   the teacher asked
them to tell   what their father did
and at her turn   she stood   mute again
because she could not bring herself to say:
      "He is dead.
       My father is dead.
       He has always been dead."

The words   were only sounds
for her memory was blank.   But they were
sounds   she could not risk.

So she stood
mute again   until the teacher asked: "Do you
have a father?" And she shook her head
     in shame
     in fear
     and sat down.

She learned   nothing they wanted her to know
but everything else
              about being alone
about keeping it close   to her heart
about silence   about how   her own words
     rebounded in her silence   about
     how she could use them
     but only   if she remained on the outside.

Grief: Brunswick Public Library, Maine

At the library   the woman
with the broken English
is broken   and so she wails
cracking   the comforting silence.

Everyone stops:
at the computers   along the orderly shelves
                            at the children's desk
where the papier-mâché animals seem
to be drained of   their colors
as if the sound   had washed them
in tears.

She clutches   a small girl
and weeps   her arms   tight around the child
while a librarian   tries to calm her.

It's an old story: her husband
left   simply left
for the West Coast   for Singapore   Canada
for a job   just down the highway   in Harpswell.

Perhaps she has no home to go to
perhaps she'll kill herself   and the child.

She wails.

The librarians huddle   and call the police
and the police   call for an ambulance.

I think about the child   her fear
the father gone   and soon the mother too.
For who will risk   her   with this woman?
Who will risk   the mother's pounding heart
her terror   her realization that she is alone
on this unfathomable continent   in a library
with so many   atlases and answers
and not one   to translate   an abandoned woman
awash in grief?

Der fremder in der fremd

Gedenkst? Do you remember
when you were a stranger
among strangers

a fremder   on papirn
a stranger   without papers?

Gedenkst di frages?

                those endless questions

Ver zayt ir?   fun vanen kumt ir?
who are you? where are you from?
why are you here   and not there?

Ver zaynen geven ayere shkheynim?
who were your neighbors? where was the school?
what work did you do? what can you do here
that you couldn't   do there?

Nokh amol for the third fourth
                              fifth time
Ver zayt ir?   fun vanen kumt ir?
who are you? where are you from?
why are you here   and not there?

Ver iz der man? ver iz di froy?
who is this man? who is this woman?
un di papirn? and their papers?
un dos kind?   and this child?
did you find it here? or bring it from there?
do you have a passport? for him? for her?
farn kind that one with the dark hair?

269

Nokh amol   for the tenth   eleventh
                                                  twelfth time
Ver zayt ir?   *Fun vanen kumt ir?*
who are you?   where are you from?
why are you here   and not there?
who do you know here?   who did you know there?
where will you sleep here?   how did you sleep there?
                                        un ayere khaloymes:
what do you dream of here?   what did you dream of there?
where will you work here?   what work did you do there?
and why can't you just   work   there?

Vu iz di vize   di grine karte   der pasport
visa?   green card?   passport?
photo?   from here   and from there?   and why did you
        cut your hair?

un dos kind?   and why did you bring
this child here   and not leave it there?

Nokh amol   for the eighteenth   nineteenth
                                                  twentieth time
ver zayt ir?   fun vanen kumt ir?
farvos zayt ir do?   un nisht geblibn dortn?
why are you here?   and why didn't you just stay there?

Acknowledgments

This collection covering fifty years of work is indebted to many.

I am most grateful to friends who have supported me for so many years, support especially needed in the years since my partner Judy's and my mother's deaths. The friendships of Cara Beckenstein, Linda Eber, Elizabeth Holtzman, Zohar Weiman Kelman, Agi Legutko, Nancy Stoller, Meredith Tax, and Vivian "Bubba" Kahan Weston have been critical in sustaining me emotionally and enabling me to continue my work. Special thanks to Elana Dykewomon for all her efforts to get me back into the stream. I am particularly grateful to Donna Gallers and Anthony Grillo for including me in their lives and for their generosity, care over my health and safety, and above all, for their company.

I am indebted to Gabi and Uwe von Seltmann, who in 2017 helped me return to Poland with a fresh perspective, introduced me to their artistic circles, and made my poetry known to a Polish audience. Since then, we have cemented our friendship, despite being separated by the Atlantic Ocean and the Covid-19 pandemic. I also want to thank Paula Sawicka for her warmth, hospitality and delicious meals, and for allowing me to use her Warsaw apartment as my base on two extended trips to Poland. Discussions with Paula, Gabi, and Uwe about the Jewish past and present in Poland became the inspiration for some of my most recent work. I also want to thank Sarah Gordon and the Adrienne Cooper Foundation for honoring me with the Dreaming in Yiddish Award, thereby making my recent trips to Poland possible.

As a poet I was a fortunate beneficiary of the (mostly unpaid) labors of countless lesbians and feminists who ran bookstores, coffeehouses, conferences and distribution centers, and who published women's newspapers and journals during the women's movement "Second Wave" in the United States. I am indebted to my co-founders and co-editors of *Conditions* magazine for helping me develop my editing skills through our collective experience of publishing a politically conscious literary magazine. I am especially grateful to Cheryl Clarke, Joan Nestle, and

Susan Sherman, my first reviewers in the late 1970s and early '80s, who made my poetry known to national feminist and lesbian audiences. Their appreciation of my poetry was a significant step towards making the present collection possible.

I want to acknowledge my indebtedness to the late Gloria Anzaldua, who first encouraged me to think about the possibilities of bilingual poetry. I am grateful to my friends Clare Kinberg, the indefatigable editor of the multicultural feminist magazine *Bridges,* and to Frieda Foreman, the indefatigable researcher and translator of women's Yiddish fiction, for encouraging my Yiddish work and offering me opportunities to publish it. Zohar Weiman Kelman honored me by including my bilingual poems in her analyses of Yiddish women's poetry.

And I am indebted to Zohar and Elana, who together with Minnie Bruce Pratt and Ellen Rifkin read the final manuscript for this collection and provided sensitive and detailed feedback. Over the past year, I received thoughtful and creative suggestions from the editors and staff of Wesleyan University Press while approaching the publication of this collection. Special thanks to Suzanna Tamminen and Jaclyn Wilson, who showed remarkable patience in helping me in the early stages of preparing the manuscript and in selecting a cover; and to Hannah Silverstein and Jim Schley, who guided me through the intricate steps of proofing and finalizing the layout of the book.

All my gratitude to Julie Enszer, poet, activist and editor of the lesbian magazine *Sinister Wisdom,* who first suggested the idea for this collection, and also to the poet Rachel Levitsky, who cheered it on. Julie, in particular, dealt with many of the details involved in initiating and completing this project. Without Julie's insistence and her ongoing support, this collection might never have seen the light of day.

Finally, I dedicate the book in memory of Judith Waterman, my partner and lifelong companion of thirty-eight years, who always maintained a belief in the importance of my work, particularly during those times when it was hardest to prioritize it. Judy's commitment to her own art and paintings and to the creative process became the model for my writing. The weight of Judy's support over so many years has become especially evident to me through its absence during the many months of preparing this collection.

Glossary

My transliteration of Yiddish, which includes *loshn koydesh* (Hebrew and Aramaic words in Yiddish), follows the rules established by YIVO Institute for Jewish Research and generally accepted by international linguistic organizations.

Arabic (A)   Hebrew (H)
French (F)   Polish (P)
German (G)   Yiddish (Y)

a nes (Y): a miracle
babcia (P): grandmother
bobe (Y): grandmother
bay undz iz es geven andersh (Y): in our home it was different
dziadek (P): grandfather
efsher an eydes (Y): perhaps a witness
erev shabes (Y): day before the Sabbath, i.e., Friday
fraytik (Y): Friday
goyim (Y): non-Jews, usually pejorative
grossaktion (G): great action; the term used by the Germans to refer to the planned deportation of Warsaw Ghetto Jews to Treblinka in the summer of 1942
herr (G): mister
Ich habe ein kleines kind (G): I have a small child
intifada (A): Palestinian uprising in the West Bank and Gaza Strip begun December 9, 1987
kadish (Y): traditional Jewish prayer for the dead
khale (Y): braided bread for the Sabbath
mame-loshn (Y): mother tongue, used synonymously to mean the Yiddish language
mitsrayim: (Y) Egypt
mitsves (Y): obligatory (good) deeds; 613 for Jewish men and 3 for Jewish women

Pan Tadeusz (P): Master Tadeusz; Poland's national verse epic by Adam Mickiewicz (1843) is required reading in Polish schools

pesakh (Y): Passover

piątek (P): Friday

rebe (Y): rabbi

rebitsin (Y): rabbi's wife

sabra (H): a native-born Israeli Jew

seder (Y): traditional Passover meal

Solidarność (P): "Solidarity" movement in Poland against Communist regime; illegal in 1983

shabes (Y): Sabbath

sheygets (Y): non-Jewish man; usually pejorative

shiva (Y): traditional Jewish seven-day mourning period for the dead

shtetl (Y): small Eastern European town with a significant Jewish population; most of these towns were completely destroyed by the end of World War II

szczęście (P): blessing

taki cud (P): such a miracle

tatuś (P): daddy

treyf (Y): non-kosher food

umschlagplatz (G): point of deportation by train for Jews being sent to concentration camps

yortsayt (Y): anniversary of a death

zaynen zey geforn kayn Treblinka (Y): they went to Treblinka

złoty, francs, marks (P, F, G): monetary units

Żyd, Juif, Jüde (P, F, G): Jew

Notes

"they're always curious"

    Although this poem does not appear in *periods of stress*, it is included here because it was written during the same period as many of the poems in that collection.

"Contexts"

    I worked on "Contexts" over a period of six months and experienced great difficulty in pulling the sections together. Only after I had read Tillie Olsen's *Silences* (New York: Dell, 1978) was I able to see the relationship between the sections and complete the poem. Both epigraphs are taken from *Silences*.

"*Bashert*"

    In the last section of this poem, "Give me my pound of flesh" echoes Shylock's demand of Antonio in Shakespeare's *The Merchant of Venice*. This is commonly cited in support of antisemitic stereotypes of Jewish avarice and greed.

"Solitary Acts"

    "To garden is a solitary act," from "The Garden" in *Claiming an Identity They Taught Me to Despise* by Michelle Cliff (Watertown, Mass.: Persephone Press, 1980).

    Neglinge: A Swedish town outside of Stockholm.

    "Like the watercolors from Buchenwald": For the extraordinary artwork produced in ghettos, concentration camps, and in hiding, see, for example, the reproductions in *Art of the Holocaust*, Janet Blatter and Sybil Milton, eds. (New York: Rutledge Press, 1981). Since 1981, there have been numerous collections documenting the art produced during the war.

"'67 Remembered"

Known also as the '67 War, Six-Day War, June War — the war between Israel and Egypt, Jordan, and Syria; the beginning of the Israeli occupation of the West Bank and Gaza Strip.

"Warsaw, 1983: *Umschlagplatz*"

"*Ikh bin nisht geven in Treblinka*" is the title poem of a collection by the Yiddish poet H. Leivik (1945).

"East Jerusalem, 1987: *Bet Shalom* (House of Peace)"

In 1987 in East Jerusalem a group of Jewish women writers (American and Israeli) met with Palestinian women to express feelings and responses to the Israeli occupation of the West Bank and Gaza Strip. I was very moved by this meeting, but did not begin writing about it until after the beginning of the first *intifada*. I was particularly affected by one of the Palestinian women, to whom this poem is dedicated.

"*Der soyne*/The Enemy: An Interview in Gaza"

I originally included "*Der soyne*" as an example of my experimentation with bilingual Yiddish-English poetry in my article "*Di feder fun harts*/The Pen of the Heart: *Tsveyshprakhikayt*/ Bilingualism and American Jewish Poetry," published in *Jewish American Poetry: Poems, Commentary, and Reflections*, eds. Jonathan N. Barron and Eric Murphy Selinger (Brandeis University Press, 2000), 320–36.

"Grief changes   and doesn't"

The epigraph, from Naomi Shihab Nye's poem "Trying to Name What Doesn't Change," is from *Words Under the Words: Selected Poems* (Portland, Oregon: Far Corner Books, 1995).

"July 22: Geology"

The Aryan Side was any place outside of the ghetto. Jews on the Aryan Side were either in hiding or passing for "Aryans" and carried Aryan papers that verified their Polish identities.

Index to Titles

'67 Remembered · 190

about my father · 18
Abutilon in Bloom · 130
aesthetic distance · 56
Aesthetics · 126
A Poem for Judy/beginning a new job · 118

Bashert · 145
between shadow and night: a treatise on loneliness · 243
blending · 48
Brooklyn, 1971: I am almost equidistant from two continents · 153

Cactus · 129
Cherry Plain, 1981: I have become a keeper of accounts · 156
Chicago, 1964: I am walking home alone at midnight · 150
conditions · 22
Contexts · 98

Dearest Friend: Regarding Esther Frumkin · 224
death camp · 17
Der fremder in der fremd · 269
Der mames shabosim/My Mother's Sabbath Days · 188
Der soyne/The Enemy: An Interview in Gaza · 216
dinosaurs and larger issues · 27
Di rayze aheym/The journey home · 174
during the war · 13

East Jerusalem, 1987: *Bet Shalom* (House of Peace) · 195
edges · 49

Entering the stream · 242

Etlekhe verter oyf mame-loshn/A few words in the mother tongue · 183

flesh is cold · 36

For Jean Swallow: whom I barely knew · 250

Fradel Schtok · 186

From the Monkey House and Other Cages · 75

Glimpses of the Outside · 132

Grief: Brunswick Public Library, Maine · 267

Grief changes and doesn't · 241

herr captain · 15

I cannot swim · 171

in between · 44

In memory of Razan al-Najjar · 217

Instructions of the dying elder · 221

it was good · 35

Jamaica Wildlife Preserve: September · 258

July 22: Geology · 256

Liberation of the roses · 237

Lithops · 125

March 1939: Warsaw, Poland · 202

Millet's Flight of Crows: Five ways to view a drawing · 228

Mitsrayim: Goat Dream · 213

Mnemonic Devices: Brooklyn Botanic Gardens, 1981 · 122

My mother at 99: Looking for home · 253

my mother's loveseat · 255

Oleander · 128

Parsing the question · 234

periods of stress · 24

perspectives on the second world war · 19
Pesakh: Reynolda Gardens, Winston Salem · 210
please don't touch me · 25
Poland, 1944: My mother is walking down a road · 148
p o w s · 14

Royal Pearl · 124

Searching for My Father's Body · 3
self-dialogues · 57
Solitary Acts · 159

the fish · 41
the house · 45
The old poet and Orion · 263
The old poet tries unsuccessfully to bring . . . · 262
The old poet reconsiders acting · 260
The old poet remembers the immigrant girl · 265
The old poet's become tired · 264
These words are dedicated to those who died · 145
These words are dedicated to those who survived · 147
The Widow and Daughter · 7
they did not build wings for them · 38
they're always curious · 37
This House · 235
trees · 238
Two Sisters: Helen and Eva Hesse · 63

Warsaw, 1941: The story of her birth · 204
Warsaw, 1983: *Umschlagplatz* · 193
when the heart fails · 34
Wind chime · 240
Winter Light · 127
Work Sonnets · 104
wound: a memory · 239

About the Author

IRENA KLEPFISZ is a lesbian poet, essayist, political activist, and Yiddishist, and a practicing secular Jew. Born in 1941 in the Warsaw Ghetto, Klepfisz spent part of the war in a Polish Catholic orphanage, and part in hiding with her mother until liberation. After a three-year stay in Sweden, in 1949 they immigrated to the United States and settled in the Bronx among Yiddish-speaking Holocaust survivors who had been active Jewish Labor Bundists (Jewish socialists) in interwar Poland. Klepfisz attended New York City public schools and Workmen's Circle Yiddish *shules*, and earned her BA at the City College of New York, then her MA and PhD at the University of Chicago. For ten years, she taught college courses at the Bedford Hills Correctional Facility. She recently retired after twenty-two years of teaching Jewish Women's Studies at Barnard College.

Klepfisz co-founded and co-edited the influential feminist magazine *Conditions*, was a member of the lesbian collective *Di vilde khayes/ The Wild Beasts*, co-founded the Jewish Women's Committee to End the Occupation, served as Executive Director of New Jewish Agenda, and organized the groundbreaking conference *"Di froyen*: Women and Yiddish," sponsored by National Council of Jewish Women.

For many years, Klepfisz served as the editor of Yiddish material for the Jewish feminist magazine *Bridges*. She is the co-editor of *The Tribe of Dina: A Jewish Women's Anthology*, and the author of *Dreams of an Insomniac* (essays) and four books of poetry, including *Keeper of Accounts* and *A Few Words in the Mother Tongue*, which was nominated for a Lambda Award.

Klepfisz has received grants in poetry from New York Foundation for the Arts and the National Endowment for the Arts. Most recently she was a recipient of the Dreaming in Yiddish Award from the Adrienne Cooper Foundation and was inducted into the Saints & Sinners Literary Festival's LGBTQ+ Writers Hall of Fame.